THE NEW GROVE
HANDEL

THE NEW GROVE
DICTIONARY OF MUSIC AND MUSICIANS
Editor: Stanley Sadie

The Composer Biography Series

BACH FAMILY
HANDEL
HAYDN
MOZART
SCHUBERT

THE NEW GROVE

HANDEL

Winton Dean

WORK-LIST

Anthony Hicks

PAPERMAC
MACMILLAN LONDON

First published in
The New Grove Dictionary of Music and Musicians,
edited by Stanley Sadie, 1980

First published in paperback 1982 by
PAPERMAC
a division of Macmillan Publishers Limited
London and Basingstoke

Associated companies in Auckland, Dallas,
Delhi, Dublin, Hong Kong, Johannesburg,
Lagos, Manzini, Melbourne, Nairobi,
New York, Singapore, Tokyo, Washington
and Zaria

ISBN 0 333 34196 1

Printed in Hong Kong

Contents

List of illustrations

GENERAL ABBREVIATIONS

A	alto, contralto [voice]	obbl	obbligato
acc.	accompaniment	orch	orchestra
add, addl	additional	orchd	orchestrated
add, addn	addition	org	organ
ant	antiphon	ov.	overture
arr.	arrangement		
aut.	autumn	perf.	performance
		pr.	printed
B	bass [voice]	pubd	published
b	bass [instrument]	pubn	publication
bc	basso continuo		
bn	bassoon	qnt	quintet
cl	clarinet	R	photographic reprint
conc.	concerto	r	recto
cont	continuo	rec	recorder
db	double bass	recit	recitative
		repr.	reprinted
edn.	edition	rev.	revision
f, ff.	folio(s)	S	soprano [voice]
facs.	facsimile	str	string(s)
fl	flute	sym.	symphony
frag.	fragment		
		T	tenor [voice]
gui	guitar	timp	timpani
hn	horn	tpt	trumpet
hpd	harpsichord	tr	treble [instrument]
inc.	incomplete	transcr.	transcription
inst	instrument		
		U.	University
Jb	Jahrbuch [yearbook]		
		v, vv	voice(s)
kbd	keyboard	v., vv.	verse(s)
lib	libretto	v	verso
		va	viola
movt	movement	vc	cello
ob	oboe	vn	violin

BIBLIOGRAPHICAL ABBREVIATIONS

AcM	*Acta musicologica*
AMw	*Archiv für Musikwissenschaft*
AMZ	*Allgemeine musikalische Zeitung*
AMz	*Allgemeine Musik-Zeitung*
AnMc	*Analecta musicologica*
CMc	*Current Musicology*
DAM	*Dansk aarbog for musikforskning*
HjB	*Händel-Jahrbuch*
JAMS	*Journal of the American Musicological Society*
JbMP	*Jahrbuch der Musikbibliothek Peters*
KJb	*Kirchenmusikalisches Jahrbuch*
MA	*The Musical Antiquary*
Mf	*Die Musikforschung*
ML	*Music and Letters*
MMR	*The Monthly Musical Record*
MO	*Musical Opinion*
MQ	*The Musical Quarterly*
MR	*The Musical Review*
MT	*The Musical Times*
PAMS	*Papers of the American Musicological Society*
PMA	*Proceedings of the Musical Association*
PRMA	*Proceedings of the Royal Musical Association*
RaM	*La rassegna musicale*
RIM	*Rivista italiana di musicologia*
RISM	*Répertoire international des sources musicales*
SIMG	*Sammelbände der Internationalen Musik-Gesellschaft*
SMw	*Studien zur Musikwissenschaft*
SMz	*Schweizerische Musikzeitung/Revue musicale suisse*
TLS	*The Times Literary Supplement*
VMw	*Vierteljahrsschrift für Musikwissenschaft*

Preface

This volume is one of a series of short biographies derived from *The New Grove Dictionary of Music and Musicians* (London, 1980). In its original form, the text was written in the mid-1970s, and finalized at the end of that decade. For this reprint, the text has been re-read and modified by the original author and corrections and changes have been made. In particular, an effort has been made to bring the bibliography up to date and to incorporate the findings of recent research.

The fact that the texts of the books in this series originated as dictionary articles inevitably gives them a character somewhat different from that of books conceived as such. They are designed, first of all, to accommodate a very great deal of information in a manner that makes reference quick and easy. Their first concern is with fact rather than opinion, and this leads to a larger than usual proportion of the texts being devoted to biography than to critical discussion. The nature of a reference work gives it a particular obligation to convey received knowledge and to treat of composers' lives and works in an encyclopedic fashion, with proper acknowledgement of sources and due care to reflect different standpoints, rather than to embody imaginative or speculative writing about a composer's character or his music. It is hoped that the comprehensive work-lists and extended bibliographies, indicative of the origins of the books in a reference work, will be valuable to the reader who is eager for full and accurate reference information and who may not have ready access to *The New Grove Dictionary* or who may prefer to have it in this more compact form.

S.S.

We are grateful to the following for permission to reproduce illustrative material: British Library, London (figs.1, 7, 10, 11, 13); The Viscount FitzHarris, Basingstoke (fig.2); Richard Macnutt, Tunbridge Wells (fig.4); Max Reis Collection, Zurich (fig.5); National Portrait Gallery, London (fig.8, cover); Moldenhauer Archives, Spokane, Washington (fig.9); Warburg Institute, University of London (fig.12).

Cover: Portrait (1756) by Thomas Hudson

1. Halle and Hamburg

George Frideric Handel* was born in Halle on 23 February 1685. He was the son of Georg Händel (1622–97), a barber–surgeon of some distinction, and his second wife Dorothea Taust (1651–1730), daughter of the pastor of Giebichenstein near Halle, and was born when his father was 63 years old. What little is known of Handel's early life is derived mainly from Mainwaring's biography, based on information received from J. C. Smith the younger and ultimately from Handel himself, but independent sources, where they exist, have often proved its chronology unreliable. The boy's interest in music declared itself early; but his father, doubtless for good pecuniary reasons, intended him for the law and forbade access to an instrument. Handel nevertheless contrived to practise secretly on a small clavichord smuggled into the attic. On one of the family visits to the court of Saxe-Weissenfels, where Handel's half-brother Karl, his senior by 36 years, held the appointment of *valet de chambre* and his father that of court surgeon, the boy's organ playing attracted the attention of the duke, who urged the reluctant father to allow his son to study music as well as law. Handel, now a student at the grammar school, was therefore placed under the tuition

---

* This was the spelling he ultimately used in England. He was baptized Georg Friederich Händel, and that spelling is the one normally used in Germany. He spelt his surname Hendel in Italy, and at first in England (which may indicate the pronunciation he expected), but later signed 'Handel' without the *Umlaut*.

of F. W. Zachow, organist of the Liebfrauenkirche at
Halle. Zachow seems to have been a gifted and sympathetic teacher. He had a large collection of German and
Italian music in manuscript, and encouraged his pupil to
copy as well as to imitate different styles. He may have
sown the seeds of Handel's lifelong habit of borrowing
and reworking old material. A volume of Handel's
copies, dated 1698, is known to have survived until the
late 18th century. He made rapid progress under
Zachow, learning the organ, harpsichord and violin as
well as composition, harmony and counterpoint, and
was encouraged to write cantatas for the church services, though none has survived.

According to Mainwaring Handel and his father paid
a visit to the court of the Electress Sophia Charlotte of
Brandenburg at Berlin, where the boy met Giovanni
Bononcini and Attilio Ariosti and made such an impression that the elector proposed to take him into his
service and send him for further instruction to Italy, an
offer declined on account of his father's failing health.
That cannot be literally true, since Ariosti did not reach
Berlin until after Georg Händel's death in February
1697, and Bononcini not until 1702. There may however have been more than one visit. On 10 February
1702 Handel matriculated at the University of Halle; he
did not join any special faculty, but may have continued
his law studies for a time. A month later, on 13 March,
he was appointed organist at the Calvinist Cathedral
(although himself a Lutheran) in succession to J. C.
Leporin, a dissolute character to whom he had been
acting as assistant. The appointment was for a prob-
ationary period of one year at a salary of 50 thaler and
free lodging. Soon after it expired, in spring or summer
1703, Handel left Halle for Hamburg; in Mainwaring's

words, 'it was resolved to send him thither on his own bottom, and chiefly with a view to improvement'. His friendship with Telemann, then a student at Leipzig, dates from these early days at Halle. Telemann recorded later that Handel was clearly a person of consequence, and the two often exchanged ideas by correspondence or in person.

Hamburg, which was an important commercial and cultural centre, possessed the only regular opera company in Germany outside the courts. Its controlling spirit was the gifted but mercurial and intemperate Reinhard Keiser, with whom Handel's relations presently became strained. The young musician found a post among the ripieno second violins at the opera, and later as a harpsichordist; he augumented his income by giving private lessons, among others to the son of the English Resident John Wyche. He soon made friends with the composer, singer and theorist Johann Mattheson, his senior by nearly four years, and for a time enjoyed free board at his father's house. Mattheson later claimed to have introduced Handel into the city's musical circles and helped him with his compositions, including *Almira* 'scene by scene'. According to him Handel was already an accomplished organist but ignorant of melodic writing before he went to the opera: 'he knew how to compose practically nothing but regular fugues'. In August 1703 the two young musicians visited the aging Buxtehude at Lübeck with a view to succeeding him as organist of the Marienkirche, but since one of the conditions was that the candidate should espouse Buxtehude's daughter, who was not in her first youth, both (like J. S. Bach two years later) prudently declined. Handel's friendship with Mattheson was briefly interrupted in December 1704 by a quarrel,

leading to a duel, over the continuo accompaniment of
Mattheson's opera *Cleopatra*. The *St John Passion* performed on 17 February 1704, long regarded as
Handel's earliest important work, has been attributed
recently to Georg Böhm and to Mattheson. Handel's
first two operas, *Almira* and *Nero*, were produced within
a few weeks on 8 January and 25 February 1705. The
first was a considerable success (the libretto ran to three
editions) and gave rise to a lively burst of pamphlet
warfare, in which literary rather than musical matters
took precedence; the second, whose music is lost, was a
failure. Keiser's hostility to a potential rival can be
discerned in his choice of the same two subjects within
the next 18 months, *Octavia* in August 1705, *Almira* in
autumn 1706, the latter on an altered version of the
libretto used by Handel. It seems however that Keiser
had first treated the subject at Weissenfels in 1704. The
score of *Octavia* served Handel as a fruitful source of
ideas for development, not only in Italy but in England
as late as the 1730s, in *Orlando* and *Ariodante*. Keiser's
opposition or the failure of *Nero* seems to have hindered
Handel's career in the theatre, although he composed one
more opera for Hamburg. This was subsequently
divided into two, *Florindo* and *Daphne*, produced in
January 1708, some time after Handel had left for Italy.
Four movements survive in fragmentary form without
their voice parts; several dances and instrumental
'choruses' also probably belong to this opera.

Almira is the only surviving major work that can be
positively identified with the Hamburg period. Though
strongly influenced by Keiser (especially in orchestration) and Mattheson, it has flashes of invention and
dramatic power, despite the prolix libretto in a mixture
of Italian and German, a regular practice at the

Hamburg opera. The style is mixed, drawing on the French tradition for the dances and Italian comedy for the servant Tabarco, the only *buffo* character in Handel's operas before Elviro in *Serse*, as well as the stiff gait of the north German cantata. The arias are often primitive and unbalanced in design, the vocal writing constricted and instrumental; there is little sign of the later melodic freedom.

Handel is said to have composed many sonatas in Hamburg, and Mattheson mentioned interminable arias and cantatas, weak in melody but strong in harmony and counterpoint. It is likely that a number of his surviving keyboard and instrumental works date from this period, even if they were revised later. Two personal characteristics are also perceptible, a sturdy independence of spirit and, in Mattheson's words, 'a natural inclination to dry humour'.

2. Italy

When he was in Hamburg Handel met Prince Ferdinando de' Medici, son and heir of the Grand Duke of Tuscany, who was impressed by his talents and invited him to visit Italy, and particularly Florence. It is doubtful if he financed the journey. According to Mainwaring Handel 'resolved to go to Italy on his own bottom, as soon as he could make a purse for that occasion', and it is likely that his principal object was to gain experience, especially of Italian opera. Mattheson said he travelled with one Binitz. Research (by Ursula Kirkendale and Reinhard Strohm) has thrown fresh light on the chronology of Handel's years in Italy. There is no reason to doubt Mainwaring's statement that he went at once to Florence (autumn 1706). His first Italian opera, generally known as *Rodrigo*, was produced there at the Cocomero Theatre probably in November 1707 under the title *Vincer se stesso è la maggior vittoria*. The opera is said to have brought Handel 100 sequins and a service of plate from the grand duke, and the favours of the prima donna Vittoria Tarquini (the grand duke's mistress), whom he was to encounter again in Venice. Tarquini did not sing in *Rodrigo*, but Handel could have met her in 1706, when she appeared in Alessandro Scarlatti's *Il gran Tamerlano* at Pratolino. He returned to Florence each autumn until 1709, made contact with the prince's court poet Antonio Salvi, several of whose librettos he was to set later in London, and probably heard G. A. Perti's operas *Dionisio rè di Portogallo* (1707), *Ginevra principessa di Scozia* (1708) and *Berenice* (1709), all on librettos by Salvi.

Handel's signature, dated Rome 1706, in a copy of Steffani's duets in the British Museum suggests that he reached that city before the end of the year (unless it refers to the old-style year ending in March 1707). He was probably the 'Sassone' mentioned by Valerio as playing the organ in the church of St John Lateran in January 1707. About this time (certainly before May) he composed his first oratorio, *Il trionfo del Tempo e del Disinganno*, to words by Cardinal Benedetto Pamphili. This may have been performed at the palace of Cardinal Pietro Ottoboni, a prominent patron of the arts. A third cardinal, Carlo Colonna, was another of Handel's noble acquaintances; but it was a rich and ambitious layman, Marquis (later Prince) Francesco Ruspoli, who elicited by far the greatest number of his Roman compositions. Ruspoli employed Handel as household musician at his palace in Rome or his country estates at Vignanello and Cerveteri at three different periods, May–October 1707, February–May 1708 and July–November 1708, and possibly in 1709 as well. The terms of his employment were flexible: he had no regular salary but was expected to supply cantatas (secular) for weekly performance on Sundays, as Bach did later under different circumstances at Leipzig. Among the other musicians in Ruspoli's household during Handel's employment were at least four who subsequently followed him to London, the soprano Margherita Durastanti, the violinists Domenico and Pietro Castrucci (father and son) and the cellist Filippo Amadei. Handel's compositions for Ruspoli include the oratorio *La Resurrezione* (April 1708), three Latin motets (performed at Vignanello in June 1707), eight or more cantatas with upper instruments – among them *Diana cacciatrice* (May

1707), *Armida abbandonata* (June 1707), *Arresta il passo* (July 1708, composed for a concert of the Arcadian Academy) and *O come chiare e belle* for three voices and orchestra including trumpet (September 1708) – the cantatas with Spanish and French words (both September 1707), and at least 40 continuo cantatas. These include the famous *Lucrezia* and *Hendel non può mia musa* (August 1708) with words by Cardinal Pamphili comparing the composer favourably with Orpheus. The principal soprano parts in nearly all these cantatas were composed for Durastanti.

The production of *La Resurrezione* in April 1708 – it had three rehearsals and two performances, on 8 and 9 April – was spectacular. A special theatre with scenery and a curtain was constructed in Ruspoli's palace, and an exceptionally large orchestra engaged, numbering at least 45 players, under the leadership of Corelli. The audiences were substantial, and 1500 copies of the libretto were printed. Durastanti sang Maddalena on the first night but was replaced by a castrato on the second by order of the pope, who objected to the appearance of a female singer in what was virtually an opera in all but name. Ruspoli's food bills reflect one characteristic for which Handel became notorious in England – his voracious appetite.

On his first sojourn in Rome, between April and July 1707, Handel composed the three most ambitious of his Latin church works, the psalms *Dixit Dominus*, *Laudate pueri* (in D) and *Nisi Dominus*. James Hall plausibly suggested that they formed part of a complete setting of the Carmelite Vespers for the feast of the Madonna del Carmine on 16 July 1707. After the production of *Rodrigo* at Florence Handel seems to have spent winter 1707–8 at Venice, where he probably

heard Alessandro Scarlatti's *Mitridate Eupatore* and
Caldara's *Partenope* and made the acquaintance of
Domenico Scarlatti and Cardinal Vincenzo Grimani,
owner of the S Giovanni Grisostomo theatre, who wrote
the libretto of *Agrippina* for him. He was at Naples for
about ten weeks from May to July 1708, when he
composed the serenata or cantata *Aci, Galatea e
Polifemo* for a ducal wedding. In winter 1708–9 he was
probably back in Rome, where alone during these years
he could have encountered the influential priest–
diplomat–composer Agostino Steffani, who was in the
service of the Elector Palatine at Düsseldorf; Handel
may have met him before, at Hanover early in 1703.
Between March and November 1709, though perhaps
not continuously, he was again at the court of Prince
Ferdinando of Tuscany. According to F. M. Mannucci,
writing in February 1711, a motet by him, *Il pianto di
Maria*, was performed at Siena on Good Friday (29
March) that year; but the music, though attributed to
Handel in several manuscript copies, bears little
resemblance to his style. By December he was in
Venice, where he won a great popular success with
Agrippina, produced on 26 December or soon after and
performed 27 times during the carnival season.

The Italian years were decisive in Handel's career.
Italy was the home not only of opera, oratorio and
chamber cantata but of the principal instrumental forms,
the concerto and the sonata. Apart from France, which
nourished its own culture and traditions, the rest of
Europe was provincial by comparison. Handel met all
the leading practitioners: Alessandro and Domenico
Scarlatti, Caldara, Corelli and probably Pasquini at
Rome (all moved in the same circles and served the
same patrons, especially Ottoboni), Lotti, Gasparini,

Vivaldi and Albinoni at Venice, Perti at Florence. Handel's keyboard contest with Domenico Scarlatti at Ottoboni's palace is famous; both were outstanding harpsichordists, but everyone, including Scarlatti, acknowledged Handel's superiority on the organ. The contest, unlike others of the kind, led to friendship and mutual admiration.

According to Mainwaring Handel composed 150 cantatas in Rome 'besides Sonatas and other Music'. That may well be true; Chrysander published 100 cantatas (72 with continuo only, the rest with other instruments), about a dozen have been discovered since, and some are doubtless lost. All but a very few belong to

1. Autograph MS of the close of Act 1 scene ii, and opening of scene iii, of Handel's opera 'Agrippina', composed 1709

the Italian years. Together with the two operas, two oratorios, *Aci, Galatea e Polifemo*, a few chamber duets and trios and the Latin psalms and motets they represent a formidable body of work. While Handel often drew on this material later, and nearly always improved it, and while some of it shows him still learning his trade and fumbling towards control of his means of expression, a great many of his Italian compositions are masterpieces in their own right, equalling and sometimes surpassing his models. This applies particularly to *Agrippina*, *La Resurrezione* and such cantatas as *Lucrezia*, *Apollo e Dafne*, *Armida abbandonata* and *Agrippina condotta a morire*. He arrived in Italy a gifted but crude composer with an uncertain command of form, and left it a polished and fully equipped artist. The most important lesson he learnt there, chiefly from the operas and cantatas of Alessandro Scarlatti, was the command of a rich, free and varied melodic style, long-breathed but rhythmically flexible, which distinguished all his later music. With it he won an absolute mastery of the technique of writing for the voice. The warm climate of Italian lyricism melted the stiffness and angularity of his German heritage, and at the same time refreshed his counterpoint; the choral movements in the Latin psalms (though there is little with which to compare them from the Hamburg period) show much of the power and euphony of their successors in the English oratorios. No doubt he learnt much from the example of Legrenzi, Caldara and other composers of the Venetian school. His harmonic idiom at this period is sometimes contorted; dissonances are more frequent and haphazard than in his later work, where he reserved them for moments of special emotional tension. His writing for strings undoubtedly benefited from his acquaintance with Corelli, though few if any purely instrumental works can be dated to these years. The fact that Handel composed only two operas in Italy was due (at least in part) to his long residence in Rome, where opera was forbidden by papal decree. Italian composers evaded the ban by composing oratorios and cantatas in a purely operatic style, and Handel followed their example. His longer cantatas with more than one character, such as *Apollo e Dafne*, are in effect one-act operas, as is also *Aci, Galatea e Polifemo*; *La Resurrezione* with its bravura vocal writing, brilliant scoring and secular treatment of character is stylistically indistinguishable from opera; the cantatas for one voice, like most of Scarlatti's, are operatic scenas. Handel was thus able, without writing much for the public theatre (though he doubtless attended it whenever he could), to digest and assimilate the idiom of Italian opera, of which Scarlatti was the most distinguished living exponent. *Agrippina*, one of the last works Handel wrote in Italy, was in every sense the climax of his career up to the age of 25.

3. Hanover and London

Handel made some useful contacts in Venice. He probably met Prince Ernst August of Hanover, brother of the elector (the future King George I of England), on his first visit in winter 1707–8. Either then or two years later he encountered Baron Kielmansegge, the elector's Master of the Horse, and the Duke of Manchester, the English ambassador. Both pressed him to visit their respective countries, and he may have been promised a post at the Hanoverian court. The Crown Prince of Tuscany had already (9 November 1709) recommended him to Prince Carl von Neuburg, Governor of the Tyrol, at Innsbruck. Handel left Italy in February 1710 and was in Innsbruck by early March, but did not avail himself of the governor's offer of employment. Instead he travelled on to Hanover, where on 16 June he was appointed Kapellmeister to the elector at a salary of 1000 thaler. One of the conditions was that he should have an immediate 12 months' leave of absence in London, which seems to have been already his principal objective; no doubt the elector, as heir to the English throne, knew that he was only transferring Handel from one of his pockets to another. Steffani, who had himself been the elector's Kapellmeister, held an ecclesiastical post at Hanover and was a staunch admirer of Handel, certainly helped him to obtain this appointment. By late July Handel was at Düsseldorf, where he spent several weeks; the Elector Palatine and the electress expressed great satisfaction with him and his playing in letters to the Crown Prince of Tuscany, the electress's brother, and she consulted him about a harpsichord for the court at Florence. In September he left Düsseldorf for London, travelling via the Netherlands.

Handel's first visit to London lasted about eight months. He was favourably received at Queen Anne's court, where he gave at least one concert (a Russian diplomat reported that his writing for trumpets made a sensation); but his eyes were on Vanbrugh's new opera house, the Queen's Theatre in the Haymarket. Its young manager, the dramatist Aaron Hill, drafted the scenario of an opera and gave it to the theatre poet, Giacomo Rossi, to versify. This was *Rinaldo*, the first Italian opera specially composed for London; it was produced on 24 February 1711 and given 15 times up to June. It was a sensational success, and a decisive influence on Handel's subsequent career. Hill went to great trouble and expense over scenery and machines; the large cast included three alto castratos led by the famous Nicolini in the title role. Handel also made special efforts, notably in the orchestra, which was reinforced for the occasion and included four trumpets and drums; but Rossi's remark that Handel finished the score in a fortnight and outran his supply of words is less impressive than it sounds, for a high proportion of the music had been composed for other purposes in Italy and some arias were incorporated with their original words. A discordant note in the chorus of praise came from the new periodical *The Spectator*, in which Addison and Steele ridiculed Hill's scenic effects (among them the provision of live sparrows to people Almirena's grove); but they were prejudiced witnesses, for Addison's English opera *Rosamond* had been a resounding failure and Steele had financial interests in the straight theatre.

John Walsh the elder published the songs from *Rinaldo* in April; apart from the anonymously issued music for *The Alchymist* (July 1710) this was Handel's first music in print, and his first association with the firm whose fortunes he largely made (Hawkins said Walsh cleared £1500 from *Rinaldo*). During this visit Handel met J. J. Heidegger, the Swiss assistant manager of the opera, who introduced him to many people in society and to the ten-year-old Mary Granville (later Pendarves, then Delany), a lifelong admirer and friend. According to Hawkins Handel played regularly at private concerts given by Thomas Britton (*d* 1714), a musical coal merchant, in his house at Clerkenwell.

Handel left London about the beginning of June 1711 and spent a few days at Düsseldorf, where the Elector Palatine detained him, explaining to his colleague at Hanover that he needed his opinion on some instruments. Handel's duties for the next 15 months were confined to chamber and orchestral music; there was no opera at Hanover. The so-called Hanoverian duets with continuo accompaniment are said to have been written at this time for Princess Caroline of Ansbach (later Queen Caroline of England, Handel's patron and friend); and according to Mainwaring Handel composed a 'variety of other things for voices and instruments'. These probably included instrumental concertos and overtures, for there was a good concert orchestra of 18 players, some of them French (they received higher salaries than their German colleagues). In November Handel went to Halle for the christening of his niece and eventual heir, Johanna Friderica Michaelsen, to whom he stood godfather. He doubtless visited his mother and Zachow at the same time, if he had not (as Mainwaring asserted) done so on his journey across Germany the previous year. His intention was certainly to return to London: a letter of July 1711 shows that he was studying English and in touch with the poet John Hughes, whose short cantata *Venus and Adonis*, probably composed about this time, was his first setting of English words. In autumn 1712 he obtained permission from the elector to make the journey 'on condition that he engaged to return within a reasonable time' (Mainwaring).

Back in London, he spent some months at the home of a Mr Andrews, whose chief residence was at Barn Elms (Barnes) in Surrey, and then three years (1713–16) with the young Lord Burlington at Burlington House in Piccadilly. Here he settled into a comfortable routine, such as he had doubtless enjoyed with Ruspoli and Ottoboni at Rome, composing during the day and playing for the company in the evenings. Burlington was already a prominent patron of the arts, and included Pope, Gay and Arbuthnot in his circle. Handel must have met them and other men of distinction; Pope had no ear for music, but Arbuthnot possessed some musical talent and became a friend and ardent supporter of Handel. Four more operas date from these years: *Il pastor fido* (completed in London on 24 October 1712 but like *Rinaldo* containing much music transferred from earlier works; produced at the Queen's Theatre on 22 November), *Teseo* (finished 19 December, produced 10 January 1713), *Silla* (privately produced, possibly at Burlington House, on 2 June 1713) and *Amadigi di Gaula* (produced 25 May 1715). The librettos of *Teseo* and *Amadigi* were dedicated to Burlington; the latter is specifically mentioned as having been composed at Burlington House. They were not uniformly successful, partly no doubt because Nicolini was absent until May 1715. In 1712 Owen Swiney (or MacSwiney) had succeeded Hill as manager of the theatre. He mounted *Il pastor fido* with old costumes and scenery, reserving the machines and 'all the Habits new & richer than the former' for the magic opera *Teseo*; but after the second night he decamped with the box-office takings to Italy. Heidegger succeeded him, and remained in charge, alone or jointly, for more than 30 years. *Il pastor fido* was a failure, *Teseo* with 13 performances a comparative success, though Handel never revived it. *Rinaldo* however enjoyed several revivals during these years, including one while Handel was at Hanover. It had more performances in London (53) than any of his other operas during his life. Little is known about *Silla*, though a recently discovered libretto has supplied the name of the author (Rossi) and the date of performance. Handel re-used much of the music in *Amadigi*, whose libretto (like that of *Teseo*) was adapted from a French original. It was given a spectacular production, 'with variety of Dancing' and 'a great many Scenes and Machines' (as a result of which the privilege of access to the stage was denied to subscribers); but the illness of a singer, a spell of very hot weather and (in July) the Jacobite rebellion shortened the season.

It was not long before Handel's operas reached Germany. *Rinaldo* was produced at Hamburg in November 1715, followed by *Amadigi* in 1717 and *Agrippina* in 1718. Nearly all the operas of the Royal Academy period (1720–28), and some later works, were staged at Hamburg, Brunswick or Wolfenbüttel (sometimes in different arrangements) within a year or two of their London premières. They were generally sung with the arias in the original Italian and new recitatives in German translation; sometimes Keiser, Telemann, Schürmann or another composer incorporated arias of his own.

The year 1713 saw Handel's introduction to English church and ceremonial music as the result of a direct commission from the queen, who bestowed on him a pension of £200. Whether or not this was designed to detach him from his Hanoverian connection, that was its effect: instead of returning 'within a reasonable time' he considerably outstayed his leave. He completed the Utrecht *Te Deum* on 14 January 1713, the *Jubilate* and the *Ode for Queen Anne's Birthday* (6 February) soon after. The Treaty of Utrecht was not signed until 31 March, but Handel's music was rehearsed before a large paying audience at the Banqueting House in Whitehall on 19 March; the official performance was in St Paul's Cathedral on 7 July. In all three works Handel modelled himself closely on Purcell, as he had used Scarlatti for his Italian cantatas. At this period Handel often played on the new Father Smith organ at St Paul's, of which he held a high opinion, before adjourning to the nearby Queen's Arms Tavern for further musical and other refreshment. He seems to have been introduced to Richard Brind, the organist, by his articled pupil Maurice Greene, who was to succeed him in 1718. In later years Handel's relations with Greene became strained, either because the latter paid court to Bononcini or because he was preferred to Handel as organist and composer to the Chapel Royal in 1727.

On 1 August 1714 Queen Anne died and was succeeded by the Elector of Hanover as George I. According to a famous story, first related by Mainwaring, the truant and chastened Kapellmeister, afraid to appear at court, was reconciled to his master by the ingenious diplomacy of his old friend Baron Kielmansegge. When the king and his court took an excursion by barge on the Thames, Kielmansegge organized a second barge containing musicians under Handel's command, whose music so captivated the monarch that he pardoned the delinquency and restored Handel to favour. Hawkins repeated the story, but said that the reconciliation was effected by Geminiani, who on settling in London in 1714 composed a set of violin sonatas dedicated to Kielmansegge; when they were played at court, he insisted that Handel alone was capable of accompanying him on the harpsichord. The water party may have been confused with a well-authenticated event of 17 July 1717, when king and courtiers, followed by a large number of boats, sailed from Whitehall to Chelsea, where they had supper, and returned by the same route at 3 a.m. At the king's particular request Kielmansegge organized at his own expense a second barge containing 50 musicians (strings as well as woodwind and brass), who played music specially composed by Handel. According to an account written two days later, 'His Majesty approved of it so greatly that he caused it to be repeated three times in all, although each performance lasted an hour – namely twice before and once after supper'. Handel almost certainly composed music for more than one such occasion. But it is unlikely that he was ever out of favour; a *Te Deum* of his composition (probably the 'Caroline') was performed at St James's in the king's presence on 26 September and 17 October 1714, and he received a half-year's salary from the Hanover treasury in October 1715. He must have realized that the death of Queen Anne, whose health was notoriously unstable, would soon confront him with his master. The king in fact doubled his pension; and a few

years later Queen Caroline raised it to £600 when
Handel undertook the musical instruction of her
daughters. This income he enjoyed for life. The
princesses were his only regular pupils in England,
though he may later have given some instruction to the
younger J. C. Smith, and the Duke of Chandos in 1724
claimed that George Monroe had been 'successful in his
Improvement' under Handel and Pepusch at Cannons.
Hawkins, denying Mattheson's statement that Babell was
a pupil, roundly declared that 'Handel disdained to teach
his art to any but princes'.

The Jacobite unrest delayed the opening of the next
opera season until February 1716, when *Amadigi* was
revived, still with Nicolini. At the performance on 20
June Handel added 'two New Symphonies', including
part of a concerto in F later published as op.3 no.4.
Early in July George I left for Hanover, and Handel
soon followed. He visited his family at Halle, where he
helped Zachow's widow, who was in straitened circumstances, and went on to Ansbach, possibly on a mission
for the Princess of Wales. There he met an old friend
from his university days at Halle, Johann Christoph
Schmidt, who was in the wool trade, and whom he
persuaded to enter his service as copyist and secretary.
Schmidt was presently followed to London by his son of
the same name; both were anglicized as John
Christopher Smith, and were closely connected with
Handel, by ties of friendship as well as business, until
the end of his life. (In a letter of 1743 the elder Smith
claimed to have served Handel for 24 years, which might
suggest that he arrived in 1719; but one of his early copies
is dated 1718.)

Handel's setting of the Passion oratorio by B. H.
Brockes is generally associated with this visit to

Germany. Keiser had set the poem in 1712, followed by Telemann in 1716 and Mattheson in 1718. Handel's work cannot be dated, since the autograph is lost. Mattheson, who implied that it preceded Telemann's, said it was composed in England and sent to Hamburg 'by post in an uncommonly close-written score'. The recent discovery of a libretto, dated Hamburg, 1716, showing a textual variant unique to Handel's setting may indicate a performance there at that date. But its first certain performance was in the refectory of Hamburg Cathedral on 23 March 1719; it was repeated there four or five times in 1720–24. Handel's most substantial setting of his native language, though inventive and mature in style, is not an artistic success. Unlike Bach, who used many of Brockes's verses in his *St John Passion*, Handel was not inspired by the sentimental imagery of German Pietism. The dramatic episodes, especially the Gethsemane scene, are splendidly realized, but the numerous commentary arias lack conviction. The spirit of the work is secular and decorative; Handel did not achieve a fusion of the German and Italian traditions, though both are present. Surprisingly in view of its prominence in the English oratorios, the chorus plays a subsidiary part; only the opening movement is developed at even moderate length. Handel's treatment of the chorales in no way rivals Bach's. He re-used some of the best music from the Passion in the oratorios *Esther*, *Deborah* and *Athalia* and the 1732 version of *Acis and Galatea*.

Handel's only other undisputed work with a German text (other than portions of *Almira*) is a set of nine German arias for soprano, melody instrument and continuo, also to words by Brockes. Their date of composition has never been determined. Chrysander proposed

1711 or 1716, Seiffert 1729. Braun showed that it must
be earlier than 1727 and suggested some time after
1724, when one of the poems was published for the first
time; the others appeared in 1721. Six of the arias,
including the setting of the poem published in 1724, use
material that also occurs in the operas *Giulio Cesare*,
Tamerlano and *Rodelinda* (1724–5), and the contexts
appear to suggest that the German versions came first. If
Handel did not compose them in 1724, when he had no
obvious links with Germany, it is just possible that he
obtained the words from Brockes privately in 1716 or
1719. There is however no reason to suppose that they
were intended as a group; differences of paper, ink and
writing in the autographs indicate that they may have
been composed over a period. The music is rich and
characteristic, despite a certain sameness in mood and
design; all but one are leisurely da capo arias.

4. Cannons

Handel probably returned to London from Germany towards the end of 1716 to supervise the revivals of *Rinaldo* and *Amadigi* in January and February 1717. For the former he composed a good deal of new music, rewriting the bass part of Argante for the German alto castrato Berenstadt. This was Nicolini's last London season and Bernacchi's first. *Amadigi* also received a new scene at its third performance (21 March). On the last night of *Rinaldo* (5 June) the French dancer Marie Sallé, a child of ten, appeared for the first time in a Handel opera. The opera house closed on 29 June and did not reopen, except for balls, concerts and French comedies, for nearly three years. During the summer Handel entered the service of the Earl of Carnarvon (from April 1719 1st Duke of Chandos), not as master of the music – Pepusch held this post during part of Handel's employment – but as resident composer. Since there is no mention of him in the London papers between the water party of July 1717 and February 1719 (apart from the performance of a new concerto at Drury Lane on 16 May 1718), he probably lived at his employer's palatial new seat at Cannons, near Edgware, with occasional visits to his town house in Albemarle Street. This was a return to his mode of life with Ruspoli and Burlington. Chandos kept a band of musicians, singers and instrumentalists, who doubled with various household duties, and built a private chapel, though this was not opened until 29 August 1720. He told Arbuthnot (25 September 1717) that Handel had

already composed four anthems and was at work on two
more 'and some Overtures to be plaied before the first
lesson'. The total number of Chandos anthems was 11,
including an arrangement of the Utrecht *Jubilate*. The
other important works composed for Cannons were the
Chandos *Te Deum* in B♭ and two English masques, *Acis
and Galatea* (spring 1718, when a guest in the house
described it as 'a little opera') and the first version of
Esther, possibly entitled *Haman and Mordecai*. One
score gives 'London, 1718' as the place and date of
composition. When revived later in London, however, it
was said to have been composed in 1720, which would
imply that Handel returned to Cannons that summer
after the first opera season of the Royal Academy of
Music.

The Cannons works have certain peculiarities of
layout. They make almost no use of the viola or the alto
voice (though the first of the three tenors in the *Acis and
Galatea* choruses and the *Te Deum* may have been a
countertenor), doubtless because such facilities were
seldom available. Nothing is known about the performance of the masques. They were probably intended for
some simple form of staging; *Acis and Galatea* is
closely modelled on the masques of Pepusch, Galliard
and others, produced repeatedly and with evident
success at Drury Lane and Lincoln's Inn Fields during
1715–18. The connection with Purcell's masques is
remote, but his influence is apparent in the music,
especially when it approaches the climate of *Dido and
Aeneas* towards the end. Handel as usual assimilated
what was best in the music of the country where he
happened to be. Though composed for small forces – it
can be performed by five singers and seven instruments
– *Acis and Galatea* is distinguished by rich melodic and

harmonic invention, the utmost refinement of texture, and a feeling for character that ranges from pastoral relaxation to profound tragedy (the death of Acis) and grotesque humour (Polyphemus). Handel's insight into human joy and suffering, apparent in the early operas and cantatas, here produced a masterpiece of singular perfection. The Cannons *Esther*, on a clumsy adaptation of Racine's tragedy, is much more uneven, though it contains music of similar power and freshness, including an aria with obbligato harp part composed (it is said) for the younger Powell. The choruses of both works look forward to the strength and variety of the English oratorio; it was Handel's revival of them as altered in 1732 that laid the foundations of the later form.

The Chandos anthems have suffered from the circumstances of their origin. They were composed for the English equivalent of a small German court, and reflect at once the urbane worldliness of 18th-century Anglicanism and the mixture of intimacy and ducal pomp at Cannons. They are too elaborate for the cathedral repertory, and have little in common with the personal religion of Bach's church cantatas; there was nothing of the mystic in Handel's personality. The style of the music is eclectic: the Purcellian anthem, the Italian sonata (in the instrumental introductions), the ringing counterpoint of Venetian church music, the German chorale – all make their contribution. The results are wholly Handelian and full of expressive and pictorial invention, though not every anthem is even in quality or balance. Handel used many of the ideas in other works, vocal and instrumental, and rewrote several Chandos anthems for the larger forces of the Chapel Royal.

5. Royal Academy

During the winter of 1718–19, several of the leading members of the nobility, under the patronage of the king, started a movement to establish Italian opera in London on a long-term basis. The money was to be raised by subscription; a payment of £200 entitled a subscriber to permanent tickets at the King's Theatre. The enterprise was known as the Royal Academy of Music. Vanbrugh in February 1720 said that almost £20,000 had been promised; the figure of £50,000 given by Burney and Hawkins is certainly exaggerated. Handel became the musical director, Heidegger the manager, Paolo Rolli Italian secretary and librettist, and Roberto Clerici scenic designer and machinist; Pope was asked 'to propose a Seal with a Suitable Motto to it', but omitted to do so. The finest singers in Europe were to be engaged, and a warrant from the governor (who was also Lord Chamberlain), dated 14 May 1719, authorized Handel to obtain them from 'Italy Germany or such other Place or Places as you shall think proper'. That his journey had been planned earlier is clear from a letter to his bereaved brother-in-law M. D. Michaelsen, dated 20 February; Handel's sister had died in July the previous year. He also wrote to Mattheson on 24 February, taking a splendidly empirical attitude towards solmization and the Greek modes but (unhappily for posterity) refusing to supply an autobiographical sketch.

Handel left London in late May, visited the Elector Palatine's court at Düsseldorf, where he may have engaged the castrato Benedetto Baldassari, and stayed with his relatives at Halle; it was on this occasion that Bach, travelling from Cöthen, narrowly missed him. By mid-July he was in Dresden, whence he wrote a brief report to Lord Burlington, one of the directors of the Academy. He stayed at Dresden several months, playing at the King of Saxony's court (for which he received a late payment of 100 ducats the following February) and renewing his acquaintance with Lotti, whose opera *Teofane* was produced with much pomp in September in honour of the electoral prince's marriage to an Austrian archduchess. Handel undoubtedly heard it and retained a copy of the libretto, which was later adapted for his own *Ottone*. Among the singers in *Teofane* were the castratos Berselli and Senesino and Handel's old acquaintances Durastanti and Boschi. All were subsequently engaged for London (the last three sang the same parts in *Ottone* as in *Teofane*), but perhaps for contractual reasons only Durastanti came for the first Academy season. The directors were particularly anxious to secure Senesino: Handel was asked to engage him 'as soon as possible . . . and for as many Years as may be', and when negotiations hung fire Heidegger and Giuseppe Riva, the Modenese representative in London, were called in. On 30 November 1719 the directors appointed Handel 'Master of the Orchestra with a Sallary' (it is not known how much) and decided to approach Giovanni Bononcini in Rome 'to know his Terms for composing and performing in the Orchestra'.

The Academy opened on 2 April 1720 with Giovanni Porta's *Numitore* (from which Handel borrowed several ideas in *Samson* more than 20 years later). Handel's *Radamisto*, dedicated to the king, followed on 27 April and was received with immense enthusiasm. Richard Meares published the score by subscription at the end of

2. Handel: portrait by Philippe Mercier

the year, with a 14-year copyright privilege that Handel had obtained on 14 June. That however afforded little protection against pirates, and was dropped after 1724. Much has been written about Handel's relations with publishers. The decisive fact was the ease with which the unscrupulous tribe, eager to profit from the work of a popular composer, found ways to puncture the leaky law of copyright. Handel seems to have confided the scores of each of his Academy operas, which were printed almost complete except for recitatives, to a single publisher: *Radamisto* to Meares, *Floridante*, *Ottone* and *Flavio* to Walsh & Hare, and the next eight to John Cluer. But he could not prevent their rivals from obtaining excerpts and selling them as 'favourite songs'; sometimes several rival selections appeared in quick succession. Walsh may in the end have obtained Handel's suffrage simply because he was the most persistent and successful, though his collections of the overtures in parts while other houses were issuing the scores seem to have had Handel's authority. The operas were also published in arrangements for flute (sometimes two flutes) and continuo, and excerpts appeared on single sheets, as supplements to other works, and in miscellanies. One of the most popular was Cluer & Creake's small-format *Pocket Companion for Gentlemen and Ladies*; the second volume (December 1725) contained many Handel items, some of which had not appeared elsewhere.

The Academy's first season was given with a makeshift company; the *Radamisto* cast of seven contained only three foreigners. With the arrival of the castratos Senesino and Berselli and the composer Giovanni Bononcini in autumn 1720 the enterprise moved into its stride and initiated a period of high artistic distinction.

For some eight years London became the operatic centre of Europe, with the best composers, the best singers, and creditable scenic designers. For a time even the finances showed a profit; a dividend of 7% was declared in February 1723, and the theatre was redecorated that summer. The second season had opened on 19 November 1720 with Bononcini's *Astarto*, which had 24 performances – more than Handel ever achieved in a single run. *Radamisto* was revived on 28 December with a new and much stronger cast, and the music almost entirely rewritten or transposed. This was Senesino's first – and very successful – appearance in a Handel opera, in a part composed for Durastanti. The Academy's third composer was the cellist Filippo Amadei (Ariosti, who had been in London earlier, did not return until early 1723). Amadei was given an opera by Orlandini to arrange, and early in 1721 was mated with Handel and Bononcini in the composite *Muzio Scevola*, each composer supplying one act and an overture. It is doubtful if this was designed as a Judgment of Paris; but when the opera was staged (15 April 1721) it was taken as such and Handel's Act 3 acclaimed (with reason) as by far the best.

The third season began in November 1721 with three revivals (successful operas, by Handel and others, were regularly revived, often with changes in the cast and fresh arias). The new operas were Handel's *Floridante* (9 December) and Bononcini's *Crispo* and *Griselda*. All three enjoyed long runs, but both of Bononcini's had significantly more performances than Handel's; indeed during his first two years in London Bononcini's operas had 63 performances against Handel's 28. This may have accounted for the latter's marked change of style from the long, elaborate and richly scored arias of *Radamisto* to the much more modest layout of his next three operas; Bononcini's simple, easily memorized melodies had captured the ear of the public. The rivalry between the composers, and still more between the factions that supported them, was already a matter of comment. The singers too had their partisans, and there were temperamental clashes within the company that eventually contributed to its demise. Rolli, a born intriguer, and his friend Senesino, who had more than his share of the vanity of public idols, clashed from the start with the imperious temper of Handel, whose treatment of singers could be dictatorial.

This was demonstrated when the much heralded Francesca Cuzzoni arrived at the end of 1722. Her refusal to sing 'Falsa imagine', her first aria in the new opera *Ottone* (12 January 1723), nearly earned her a summary defenestration from the enraged composer. The fact that Handel was right – the aria made Cuzzoni's reputation in London – may not have endeared him to the singer. Cuzzoni's success in *Ottone* was sensational; the run on tickets was likened to the South Sea Bubble, and the renewed factions led to disorders in the theatre. From this production Handel began to draw ahead of Bononcini, though his second opera of the season, *Flavio* on 14 May, made less impression. Meanwhile Ariosti had arrived and produced his first London opera, *Coriolano*, on 19 February; his popularity never rivalled that of Handel or Bononcini. In April a plan for the company to visit Paris in July was announced, with much circumstantial detail, in the London and Paris press. The scheme was mooted again the following summer, and French librettos of *Ottone* and *Giulio Cesare* were actually printed; but for reasons unknown this interesting experiment was never carried out.

The next two seasons carried Handel to the summit of his achievement as a composer of heroic *opera seria*. He produced three major masterpieces in succession: *Giulio Cesare in Egitto* (begun in summer 1723 and rewritten several times before performance) on 20 February 1724, *Tamerlano* (which also had a disturbed period of gestation) on 31 October, and *Rodelinda* on 13 February 1725. The first and third were particularly successful with the public; Cuzzoni and Senesino won great acclaim as Cleopatra and Caesar, and the former's brown silk costume as Rodelinda excited the world of fashion. This was the first opera since *Radamisto* that Handel published on subscription (eight more operas, *Alexander's Feast* and the Grand Concertos of op.6 were to follow). *Tamerlano* saw the début (as Bajazet) of the first great Italian tenor to visit London, Francesco Borosini. In these three works, as well as *Ottone* and *Flavio*, Handel's collaborator was Nicola Haym, a professional musician, whose method (under Handel's close supervision) was not to exercise his own literary wings but to adapt older Italian librettos to London taste. When he did not cut out too much he was generally successful. Rolli, dismissed or demoted by the directors of the Academy in 1722 but back in harness by 1726, had higher literary ambitions but much less dramatic competence; all his texts for Handel except *Deidamia* are broken-backed. Both librettists were active during the Academy's last three seasons.

In summer 1725 the directors decided to invite Faustina Bordoni to join the company (her engagement had been rumoured as early as March 1723). She is said to have asked £2500 for the season, but did not arrive until April 1726. Handel had meanwhile revived *Ottone* with great success on 8 February and given the first performance of *Scipione* on 12 March. Another new opera, *Alessandro*, marked the first appearance of the two prima donnas and Senesino in the same bill (5 May). According to Deutsch each of the three received £2000; Fougeroux in 1728 gave the figure as £1600. In either event it was very high, and the Academy soon found itself in financial difficulties. Its calls on the subscribers became more and more frequent, and so did the quarrels of the factions, which branched into a lively warfare of verses and pamphlets. Burney remarked drily that 'it seems impossible for two singers of equal merit to tread the same stage, *a parte eguale*, as for two people to ride on the same horse, without one being behind'. The next season did not begin until January 1727, apparently because Senesino was ill. *Admeto*, produced on 31 January with new scenery by Goupy, was a great and deserved success; it is easily the best of the five operas in which Handel had to write parts of equal prominence and effectiveness for Cuzzoni and Faustina. Quantz heard it in March and bestowed great praise on the orchestra as well as the singers, as did Fougeroux a year later. The behaviour of the audiences deteriorated during the spring; catcalls and disturbances were frequent, and reached their climax at a performance of Bononcini's *Astianatte* on 6 June, when the two prima donnas came to blows on the stage in the presence of the Princess of Wales.

The season of 1727–8 was the Academy's last. In November Mrs Pendarves described the operas as 'at their last gasp; the subscription is expired and nobody will renew it. The directors are always squabbling, and they have so many divisions among themselves that I

wonder they have not broke up before'. The
unprecedented success of *The Beggar's Opera*,
produced at Lincoln's Inn Fields on 29 January 1728
and given 62 times before the end of the season, seems
to have been rather the effect than the cause of the
troubles at the King's Theatre. Handel brought out three
new works, *Riccardo Primo* (composed the previous
spring but rewritten as a patriotic manifesto in honour
of the new king, George II) on 11 November, *Siroe* (his
first setting of Metastasio) on 17 February, and *Tolomeo*
on 30 April. The Academy finally closed its doors with
a performance of *Admeto* on 1 June.

Much of Handel's time during the Academy years
must have been taken up with administration and control of the unruly forces committed to his charge. Little
is known of any other activities, apart from his instruction of the princesses, which was first mentioned in the
press on 29 August 1724 in a report of his playing the
organ at St Paul's. In January the same year he received
£3 18s. 6d. for a new anthem (possibly the Chapel Royal
version of *Let God arise*) performed on the occasion of
George I's return from Hanover. A year earlier (25
February 1723) he had received an appointment as
composer to the Chapel Royal. In the four anthems
written for George II's coronation (11 October 1727)
Handel had the services of 47 singers and a very large
orchestra said to have numbered 160. It was an
occasion of ceremonial rather than artistic splendour:
the Archbishop of Canterbury noted against *My heart is
inditing* in the Order of Service: 'The anthems in
confusion: all irregular in the music' (this remark may
however refer to a rehearsal).

This was a time of growing fame and prosperity for
Handel; although he had probably lost money in the

South Sea Bubble, as a salaried employee and a royal pensioner he did not suffer in pocket while the Academy lasted. His music was more and more in demand at concerts and between the acts of plays; the unquenchable popularity of the Water Music dates from these years. The first recorded performance of his work in the provinces was at Bristol on 22 November 1727, when church music was sung in the cathedral and excerpts from *Acis and Galatea* and 'an Oratoria' (presumably *Esther*) in the theatre. On 13 February that year Handel had applied for English naturalization; it was granted by Act of Parliament a week later. By summer 1723 he had moved into a new house in Brook Street, near Grosvenor Square, where he lived for the rest of his life. The house still stands.

6. Second Academy; rival opera companies

Handel was not to be deterred by one commercial failure from continuing his operatic career. In January 1729 the directors of the Academy agreed to let the King's Theatre to him and Heidegger in partnership 'to carry on operas without disturbance for 5 years', and to lend them their stock of scenery, costumes and machines. The partners decided to run the opera on an annual subscription basis at 15 guineas per season ticket; according to Rolli Handel was to be paid £1000 – exactly the amount subscribed by the king. The 1728–9 season was blank, but Heidegger visited the Continent before the end of the year in search of singers, without success. He wished to engage the great castrato Farinelli and apparently both rival prima donnas, but Handel preferred to write for fresh voices. He himself left on a similar errand in early February 1729 and visited Venice, Rome (where he called on his old patron Ottoboni) and doubtless other cities. In June he was in Halle, where he saw his mother for the last time (she died in December 1730 at the age of 79) and is said to have been invited to Leipzig by Bach through his son Friedemann. Handel passed through Hanover and possibly Hamburg, returning to London on 29 June. Of his new company only the distinguished but aging castrato Bernacchi had sung in London before; the others included the soprano Strada, the contraltos Merighi and Bertolli, the tenor Fabri and the Hamburg bass

Riemschneider.

The season opened on 2 December with the new opera *Lotario*, which was not a success. Nor was *Partenope* (24 February 1730), though Handel tried a radical change of style from heroic drama to ironic comedy. He fell back on revivals, including the popular *Giulio Cesare*, and pasticcios, for which he supplied recitatives. Walsh brought out the score of *Partenope* and was henceforth Handel's regular publisher. Since the London public did not like Bernacchi, Handel was forced in the summer to negotiate for the return of Senesino. This he did through two English residents in Italy, Francis Colman, the envoy to Florence, and Owen Swiney; Senesino was secured for 1400 guineas. On 8 August Handel tried the new organ at Westminster Abbey and pronounced it 'a very curious Instrument'.

The 1730–31 season was much more propitious. After two revivals in which the public welcomed Senesino with the greatest applause, Handel obtained a considerable success with *Poro* (2 February 1731), based on Metastasio's *Alessandro nell'Indie*. He then revived *Rinaldo*, for the first time since 1717, much revised with new sets and costumes, and the popular *Rodelinda*. The following season began with three brief revivals, in which he introduced a new tenor, Pinacci, and the impressive bass Antonio Montagnana. But *Ezio* (15 January 1732) was the worst failure Handel had yet suffered (only five performances); as a result he resorted once more to *Giulio Cesare* and made drastic cuts in the recitatives of the next opera, *Sosarme* (15 February). This had some effect (the opera was 'much crowded'), but the abridgment of recitative – always a tedious nuisance in the opinion of London audiences – became so regular an expedient in new operas and revivals that

the plots were scarcely comprehensible without the sum-
maries in the printed libretto. It had already marred
some of the later Academy operas.

In spring 1732 an event took place that was to trans-
form both Handel's career and the history of music in
England. On 23 February Bernard Gates, Master of the
Children of the Chapel Royal, gave the first of three
private performances of *Esther* at the Crown and
Anchor Tavern in the Strand. This was the first oratorio
heard in London, and it was given with action, the stage
cast (mostly boys) supported in the choruses by members of the Chapel Royal and Westminster choirs 'after
the Manner of the Ancients, being placed between the
Stage and the Orchestra'. The venture was such a
success that Handel's pupil Princess Anne asked him to
transfer the production to the King's Theatre. Before
this could be done a pirated performance at the Great
Room, York Buildings, was announced for 20 April.
Handel retaliated in the only effective way by revising
and enlarging the score, 'to be perform'd by a great
Number of the best Voices and Instruments' at the
King's Theatre on 2 May. But he added: 'N.B. There
will be no Action on the Stage, but the House will be
fitted up in a decent Manner for the Audience. The
Musick to be disposed after the Manner of the
Coronation Service'. The reason for this, as Burney
learnt from two distinguished members of the Gates
cast, was that the Bishop of London, as dean of the
Chapel Royal, forbade the stage representation of a
sacred subject in the opera house, 'even with books in
the children's hands'. Handel gave six performances of
Esther in May, and they were received with great
enthusiasm, though the Cannons score had been expanded into a clumsy pasticcio and the Italian singers,

according to a contemporary account, 'made rare work with the *English* Tongue you would have sworn it had been *Welch*'.

A few days later *Acis and Galatea* suffered a similar transformation. It had been given once in London in March 1731; but in May 1732 an English opera company of which the Arnes, father and son, were the moving spirits put on two stage performances at the New Theatre in the Haymarket, right opposite the King's; the future Mrs Cibber and Gustavus Waltz played Galatea and Polyphemus. Handel reacted to this piracy in the same way: he expanded the score with numerous additions from the Naples cantata *Aci, Galatea e Polifemo* and other sources (including the *Brockes Passion*), but this time had it sung macaronically in a mixture of English and Italian. It was given with quite elaborate scenery and costumes 'and every other Decoration suited to the Subject', but no stage action. There were four performances, the first on 10 June. Although an artistic monstrosity, this production too was a success with the public. Of such dubious and fortuitous parentage was the English oratorio born.

Handel opened the 1732–3 season with a pasticcio based on Leo's *Catone in Utica* and a number of revivals, including *Acis and Galatea*. On 5 December his old associate Aaron Hill, in an eloquent letter, appealed to him 'to deliver us from our *Italian bondage*; and demonstrate, that *English* is soft enough for opera, when compos'd by poets, who know how to distinguish the *sweetness* of our tongue, from the *strength* of it'. Unhappily the appeal was vain, though Handel was soon to use English in another medium, and the Arne enterprise withered for want of the very quality Handel might have supplied. He had just finished one of his greatest operas, *Orlando*, whose production on 27 January 1733 made a great impression, visual as well as musical ('extraordinary fine and magnificent' was one comment). Its run was interrupted in March by Strada's illness, and after briefly reviving *Floridante* Handel brought out a new oratorio, *Deborah*, on 17 March. This too was largely a pasticcio, padded out with coronation anthems, and it was given with large forces ('near a hundred performers, among whom about twenty-five singers'); the *Daily Advertiser* described it as 'an Entertainment, perhaps, the most magnificent that has ever been exhibited on an English Theatre'. For the first night Handel doubled the price of tickets, an event that unfortunately coincided with Sir Robert Walpole's introduction of an unpopular Tobacco Excise Bill and offered an opening to Handel's enemies. The performance was ill-attended and Rolli published a particularly distasteful attack.

Dissension had again broken out in the opera company, chiefly through Handel's strained relations with Senesino. In January Lord Delawarr wrote to the Duke of Richmond: 'There is a Spirit got up against the Dominion of Mr Handel, a subscription carry'd on, and Directors chosen, who have contracted with Senesino, and have sent for Cuzzoni, and Farinelli . . . Porpora is also sent for'. This led to the establishment of the so-called Opera of the Nobility, which held its first meeting at Hickford's Room on 15 June at the instigation of the Prince of Wales, in traditional opposition to his father (and Handel's protector) the king. Handel seems to have dismissed Senesino, who made a farewell speech to the audience on the last night of the opera season (9 June).

Early in July Handel paid a visit to Oxford at the invitation of the university vice-chancellor. The occasion was an elaborate degree-giving ceremony known as the Publick Act. Handel is said to have been offered an honorary doctorate, but he did not accept it; he told Mizler in May 1744 that he was too busy. He gave five performances of oratorio in the Sheldonian Theatre, including the première (10 July) of the newly composed *Athalia*, and conducted the bilingual *Acis and Galatea* in Christ Church hall; some of his anthems were sung in the Sunday services at St Mary's church. He had with him the opera orchestra – denounced by a reactionary don as 'Handel and his lowsy crew . . . a great number of forreign fidlers' – but only Strada of the leading singers; the other parts were taken by lesser artists, mostly English, including Waltz and the local countertenor Walter Powell. The performances were crowded and very profitable, since large numbers of people had come to Oxford for the ceremonies.

Back in London, however, Handel's contract with Heidegger still had one year to run. He launched the 1733–4 season at the end of October, two months before the other party were ready, with a series of pasticcios and a revival of *Ottone*; his new company included the veteran Margherita Durastanti, now a mezzo-soprano, and the castratos Scalzi and Carestini. Carestini made a favourable impression, but audiences were thin and Handel obtained fewer subscribers than his rivals. The Nobility opened at Lincoln's Inn Fields on 29 December with Porpora's *Arianna in Nasso*, cast almost entirely from Handel's former company with Senesino, Montagnana, Bertolli and Gismondi, joined in April by Cuzzoni. Handel's *Arianna in Creta* – the common heroine may have been a coincidence, since he had finished his score on 5 October – came out on 26 January and received 17 performances; attendances im-

proved and Carestini was much acclaimed. In March
Handel put together a wedding anthem for the marriage
of his pupil the Princess Royal to the Prince of Orange
and a serenata, *Il Parnasso in festa*, both largely pasticcios from *Athalia*, which had not been heard in London.
The serenata was given in the theatre, with scenery but
without action, on 13 March. *Deborah* was revived (in
bilingual form), followed by *Sosarme* and *Acis and
Galatea*; but neither opera house was doing well. Porpora's *Ifigenia* was a failure; he also challenged Handel
unsuccessfully with an oratorio, *Davide e Bersabea*. On
18 May Handel produced a drastically revised version
of the old opera *Il pastor fido*, adding choruses and
some new music.

After the close of the season (6 July 1734) Heidegger
let the King's Theatre to the Nobility and Handel moved
to Rich's new playhouse in Covent Garden, opened in
December 1732. This time the Nobility obtained a
flying start (29 October) with the aid of the newly
arrived Farinelli, who created a predictable sensation.
They also invited Hasse, but he refused to come on
hearing that Handel was still alive. Handel now had the
services of a ballet company led by the distinguished
French dancer Marie Sallé, who appeared in all his
operas this season. He opened on 9 November with a
further revision of *Il pastor fido*, enlarged by dances in
each act and a one-act opera-ballet in the French style,
Terpsicore, as prologue; this work remained unique in
the London theatre. A revival of *Arianna in Creta* followed, then a Handel pasticcio, *Oreste*, and on 8
January 1735 the new opera *Ariodante*; the ballet
played a part in all three, but failed to draw the town.
The English tenor John Beard sang his first role under
Handel in *Il pastor fido*, and was joined in *Ariodante* by

the soprano Cecilia Young, later the wife of Thomas
Arne. The Nobility had retaliated in December with
Handel's own *Ottone*, in which Farinelli sang Adelberto,
his only Handel part (but without any of the original
arias), and followed it in February with Porpora's
Polifemo. In the spring Handel enlarged the scope of his
oratorio programme, which now tended to gravitate
towards Lent (though it was another ten years before the
practice became automatic), giving six performances of
Esther, three of *Deborah* and five of *Athalia* – the first in
London. The singers were English and Italian (including
Strada and Carestini); Handel supplied a fresh element
of virtuosity by playing organ concertos, specially composed for the occasion, during the intervals. He thus
created a new art form, and one that was to become
increasingly popular; concertos for organ or for
orchestra alone (sometimes double orchestra) were a
regular feature of his later oratorio seasons. He composed at least four organ concertos this spring, and in
Deborah, according to the *London Daily Post*,
inaugurated 'a large new Organ, which is remarkable for
its Variety of curious Stops; being a new Invention, and
a great Improvement of that Instrument'. On 16 April
the production of *Alcina*, one of his richest scores,
brought his last great operatic success (it was given 18
times in succession). Carestini, despite an initial jib at
the exquisite but unspectacular aria 'Verdi prati',
triumphed as the hero, and Sallé was again prominent;
but her revealing costume scandalized the audience, who
hissed her later performances. She never returned to
London.

During the summer, on his way to take the cure at
Tunbridge Wells, Handel received an oratorio libretto,
probably *Saul*, from Charles Jennens. His expenses in

3. Handel: engraving (1738) by Jacob Houbraken

the two previous seasons had greatly exceeded receipts, and when the Nobility reopened (unsuccessfully) in October 1735 he made no attempt to challenge them. Lord Hervey described how, at a performance of Veracini's *Adriano in Siria* on 25 November, 'Handel sat in great eminence and great pride in the middle of the pit, and seemed in silent triumph to insult this poor dying Opera in its agonies'. Hervey censured him for refusing to compose; but Handel had a new string to his bow. On 19 February 1736 Covent Garden saw the first performance of his setting of Dryden's ode *Alexander's Feast*, with Strada, Cecilia Young and Beard in the principal parts. It was received with acclamation, and two years later (March 1738) was published by subscription, with a portrait print by Houbraken (fig.3), in complete full score – the only important Handel work, apart from *Acis and Galatea* in 1743, to appear thus during the composer's life. Walsh paid Handel £105. After the usual spring oratorios and a new anthem for the wedding of the Prince of Wales on 27 April 1736 (Porpora produced a serenata sung by the all-star cast of Cuzzoni, Farinelli, Senesino and Montagnana, but it made little impression), Handel gave a short opera season of five weeks in May and June. A new soprano castrato, Conti, made his début on 5 May in a revival of *Ariodante*, but the principal work was *Atalanta*, a pastoral culminating in a spectacular apotheosis, with fireworks and bonfires, in honour of the Prince of Wales. This was doubtless a tactful move to propitiate a former enemy; it seems to have succeeded, for the opera was revived in November at the prince's request.

Both companies struggled on for one more season, against mounting public indifference. Handel opened first (6 November 1736) with *Alcina*, much shortened and deprived of its ballet; the Nobility (now without

Porpora) replied with Hasse's *Siroe*, in which two sopranos later associated with Handel, Chimenti and Duparc, made their London début. On 8 December Handel introduced another new castrato, Domenico Annibali, in a revival of *Poro* (Conti, Strada and Beard were still in the company); he was allowed to interpolate arias by Ristori and Vinci, one of only two occasions on which Handel permitted this in one of his own works (earlier the same year Conti introduced arias of unknown provenance into *Ariodante*). He produced three new operas this season, *Arminio* on 12 January 1737, *Giustino* on 16 February and *Berenice* on 18 May; all were failures. For the Lent oratorio period he completely rewrote his 1707 oratorio, now entitled *Il trionfo del Tempo e della Verità* (this version has never been published) and revived *Alexander's Feast*, *Il Parnasso in festa* and *Esther* (sung partly in Italian). He also prepared *Deborah*, but did not perform it, possibly as a result of the illness – whether a stroke or, as has recently been argued, a form of severe rheumatism – that partially crippled him on 13 April. His right arm was temporarily immobilized, so that he was unable to play (he could not conduct *Berenice*); his mind was also affected. In June both opera companies closed in financial ruin, the Nobility (with Farinelli singing to the end) on 11 June, Handel's with a command performance of *Alexander's Feast* on 25 June. It is not true however that he was declared bankrupt, at this time or later.

7. Opera, ode or oratorio?

Handel's activities over the next four years remained as vigorous as ever, but their multifarious nature betrays a certain indecision as to his path. He tried several, and all appeared to peter out; it was a chance invitation to Dublin that determined the issue. Perhaps the most striking feature of his career at this period is his obstinate reluctance to abandon Italian opera after it had repeatedly failed with the public. The change to oratorio, unplanned and fitfully executed, was certainly not the result of a preference for edifying subjects. But first he had to repair his health. About the beginning of September he went to Aix-la-Chapelle, accompanied by the elder Smith, to take the sulphur baths. Within six weeks they had effected a remarkable recovery; his organ playing in the nearby convent struck the nuns as a miracle. By mid-October he was at Elbing on the Baltic, where arias from his operas were arranged as a pasticcio, *Hermann von Balcke*, for the fifth centenary of the town. He returned to London at the end of the month and on 15 November began *Faramondo*; Heidegger had just opened a new season at the King's and engaged Handel as composer and conductor at a salary of £1000. However the death of Queen Caroline on 20 November closed the theatres until the end of the year. Handel was asked to compose a funeral anthem for his friend and patron; it was finished on 12 December, rehearsed in the Banqueting Hall on 14 December (the royal family were present incognito), and performed at

Westminster Abbey on 17 December. His recovery is
amply attested by the fact that he finished *Faramondo*
on 24 December, rested on Christmas Day, and began
another opera, *Serse*, on 26 December.

The production of *Faramondo* on 3 January 1738
won applause for another new castrato, Caffarelli, and
an ovation for Handel, making his first appearance in
the theatre since his illness; but the public showed more
enthusiasm for *The Dragon of Wantley*, Lampe's satire
on Italian opera. On 25 February Handel brought out
Alessandro Severo, a pasticcio from earlier works with a
little new music, and on 28 March gave a mixed vocal
and instrumental concert at the theatre for his own
benefit, announcing it as 'an Oratorio' (there were no
oratorios proper this season). This unusual course was
dictated by a desire to clear his debts; according to
Hawkins he still owed money to Strada and other singers. It was highly successful; Mainwaring put the takings at £1500, Egmont (who was present) at £1000,
Burney at £800. *Serse*, produced on 15 April, was on
the other hand a total failure. At the end of the month
Jonathan Tyers, the proprietor, at his own expense
erected a statue of Handel by Roubiliac in Vauxhall
Gardens (this was for long in the vestibule of Novello's
music shop in Wardour Street, and is now in the
Victoria and Albert Museum). About the same time a
Fund for the Support of Decayed Musicians (now the
Royal Society of Musicians) was established at a meeting at the Crown and Anchor Tavern; its statutes are
dated 8 May 1738. Handel was an original subscriber,
and subsequently gave an oratorio performance for its
benefit every spring. He also supported the Foundling
Hospital, which dates from two years later, and in due
course, like Hogarth, was elected a governor. It was

probably his well-known generosity to charitable organizations that inspired the Lord Lieutenant of Ireland to invite him to Dublin.

On 24 May Heidegger advertised for subscribers to a new opera season, but the poor response led him to renounce the plan on 25 July. On the very next day Handel began a new oratorio, *Saul*. The composition did not go easily; he temporarily dropped it in September in favour of an opera, *Imeneo*. Jennens, the librettist of *Saul*, visited him about this time and left an amusing description of his 'maggots'. There is little doubt that Handel, deprived of stage spectacle and with a company mostly of English singers (led by the Italian-trained French soprano Elisabeth Duparc, known as La Francesina), intended to take the public by storm. He used an enormous orchestra, including three trombones, carillon (a specially constructed keyed glockenspiel), a large new organ – probably a claviorganum – said to have cost £500, and the double-bass kettledrums of the artillery train, borrowed by special permission from the Tower of London. Some of these instruments, but not the trombones, appeared in later oratorio seasons. Immediately after finishing *Saul* at the end of September Handel began the choral epic *Israel in Egypt* (originally entitled *Exodus*), probably also on words compiled by Jennens, and finished it within a month. He planned to incorporate the funeral anthem in the last act of *Saul*, then used it to begin *Israel in Egypt*; hence the latter's two-act form.

Handel had hired the King's Theatre from Heidegger for 12 nights, and opened with *Saul* on 16 January 1739; Beard and Cecilia Young, now Mrs Arne, as well as Francesina were in the cast. The oratorio was well received and given six times. Revivals of *Alexander's*

Feast and *Il trionfo del Tempo* followed, and then, on 4
April, the first performance of *Israel in Egypt*; all were
supplemented by organ concertos, including two new
ones. *Israel* was a failure, partly because the use of
scriptural words in the theatre was an unwelcome
novelty (it was both attacked and defended on irrelevant
grounds) and partly because the overwhelming number
of choruses unbalanced the texture. For the second
performance it was 'shortned and Intermix'd with
Songs' (in English and Italian); but it was never popular
in Handel's life and seldom revived. On 1 May he tried a
new expedient, a pasticcio in Italian entitled *Jupiter in
Argos*, announced as 'a Dramatic Composition ...
Intermix'd with Chorus's, and two Concerto's on the
Organ'. It was given twice and forgotten.

For the next two seasons Handel took Rich's theatre
in Lincoln's Inn Fields. In September 1739 he set
Dryden's shorter *Ode for St Cecilia's Day* (much of it
based on borrowings from Muffat's *Componimenti*), followed by the 12 Grand Concertos for strings (op.6), the
last of which was finished on 30 October. Walsh at once
opened a subscription for their publication and obtained
a new privilege of copyright, that of 1720 having expired. They were issued on 21 April 1740, Handel's last
work published on subscription. They were not the only
instrumental works of his to appear in print about this
time. The first set of six organ concertos (op.4) had
come out late in 1738, allegedly in answer to a pirated
edition (no copy of which is known), followed by the
seven trio sonatas of op.5 on 28 February 1739 and the
second set of organ concertos on 8 November 1740.
Earlier, in 1734, Walsh had issued six concerti grossi as
op.3, and in 1732 had put out revised editions of two
sets of sonatas (solos, op.1, and trios, op.2),

which he had first issued with a false Amsterdam imprint shortly before.

Handel had opened his Lincoln's Inn Fields season on 22 November 1739 with the two Dryden odes in a double bill, and on 13 December revived *Acis and Galatea*, divided for the first time into two acts with a carillon part in the new chorus 'Happy we' at the end of Act 1. It was not a happy season for the arts, owing to the outbreak of war with Spain and the exceptionally severe winter, in which the Thames was frozen over and the theatres had to be temporarily closed. In such conditions, in January and February 1740, Handel composed the vernal masterpiece *L'Allegro, il Penseroso ed il Moderato*, for which Jennens again supplied the text, arranging Milton with much skill and, at Handel's request, adding a third part of his own. This was less popular than the rest, and generally dropped in later years. The work had its first performance on 27 February with two of the new op.6 concertos (all were introduced during the course of the season) and the organ concerto op.7 no.1. Single performances of *Saul*, *Esther* and *Israel in Egypt* followed. Handel's company remained the same, with no Italians. From this period his earlier oratorios and odes were played with increasing frequency at provincial festivals and London music clubs, and sometimes for the benefit of singers and charities. With the establishment of the Three Choirs, Salisbury and other festivals performances became common during Handel's life; they were given with his permission from manuscript scores supplied by J. C. Smith and his assistants. The correspondence of Lord Shaftesbury and the minute-books of the Edinburgh Musical Society give details about such transactions in later years. Smith received £7 17s. from Edinburgh for a copy of *Deborah* in 1754 and £5 7s. for *Judas Maccabaeus* in 1755. In 1756 William Hayes was allowed to borrow a score of *Joshua* for performance in Oxford, provided the manuscript was treated with care and no copy taken, 'for otherwise both Handel and Smyth (his copiest) will be injur'd'. Similar arrangements were made for the loan of the same work to Salisbury in 1757–8.

Handel visited the Continent in summer 1740; on 9 September he played the organ in a Haarlem church. On his return he made a final attempt at Italian opera, resuming work on *Imeneo* and finishing his last opera, *Deidamia*, in late November. Both failed ignominiously; *Imeneo*, announced as an 'operetta' (22 November), had two performances, *Deidamia* (10 January 1741) three. Handel had only one Italian (the castrato Andreoni) in *Imeneo* and two in *Deidamia*; but the indifference of the public rather than the quality of the artists or the music seems to have been responsible for the fiasco. The English works were scarcely more successful. *L'Allegro* was revived on 31 January with many additions, some sung in Italian, as were *Il Parnasso in festa*, *Acis and Galatea* and *Saul*. A single performance of the last was the only oratorio; it looks as if Handel despaired of the new form as well as the old. A letter in the *London Daily Post* of 4 April quoted a rumour that he meant to leave England, and appealed for support; the Earl of Egmont, who attended his last performance on 8 April, noted that he was 'intending to go to Spa in Germany'. Early in July he was composing Italian duets.

Handel's position was, however, transformed by the lord lieutenant's invitation to Dublin. It is almost certain that *Messiah*, composed in London between 22 August and 14 September 1741 on a text compiled from the

Bible by Jennens, was designed for the purpose it first served, the benefit of Dublin charities, and probable that Handel intended to perform *Samson* too in Dublin. The libretto for this had been put together skilfully by Newburgh Hamilton from *Samson Agonistes* and other poems of Milton. Handel finished the first version of the score on 29 October, saw a pasticcio at the King's Theatre, now under Lord Middlesex, two days later (he told Jennens that 'it made me very merry all along my journey') and at once left for Dublin. He travelled by way of Chester, where his ship was delayed by contrary winds and he took the chance to rehearse some of the *Messiah* choruses with local singers. Burney, then a schoolboy, met him for the first time and left an amusing description of the occasion. Handel reached Dublin on 18 November and took lodgings in Abbey Street. He was soon playing the organ and conducting some of his anthems in churches. He announced a subscription series of six 'Musical Entertainments' at Neale's new Music Hall in Fishamble Street, opened just before his arrival, with an orchestra led by his old friend Dubourg. All the tickets were quickly sold, and a second series followed, ending on 7 April 1742. Handel opened on 23 December with *L'Allegro* (he tactfully told Jennens that his words for *Il Moderato* were 'vastly admired'); the other works, all interspersed with organ and other concertos, were *Acis and Galatea* with the *Ode for St Cecilia's Day*, *Esther*, *Alexander's Feast* and a concert version of *Imeneo*, announced as a serenata. The singers included Christina Maria Avoglio and Mrs Cibber. The performances were crowded – special arrangements had to be made for access to the building – and Handel was delighted with his reception. *Messiah* was publicly rehearsed on 9 April and performed in the Music Hall

on 13 April, mostly by local singers and the choirs of
the two cathedrals; Dubourg, Avoglio and Mrs Cibber
again took part and gave their services. Once more the
reception was enthusiastic; the audience was estimated
at 700, and the three charities benefited to the extent of
about £400. By special request Handel conducted *Saul*
on 25 May (the public rehearsal 'was agreed by all the
Judges present, to have been the finest Performance that
hath been heard in this Kingdom') and repeated *Messiah*
on 3 June. The whole visit was a triumph for Handel;
his music was played and sung at many other concerts,
and for years after his departure was almost as popular
in Dublin as in London. His oratorios in particular
earned large sums for charity (he presented a score of
Messiah to the Charitable Musical Society). He left
Dublin for Chester on 13 August, intending (as he told
Jennens in September) to go back and resume his
oratorios a year later. That plan was probably abandoned because of the great success of *Samson* in
London. Handel also forwarded to Jennens a document
in which the Bishop of Elphin showered fulsome praise
on *Messiah* and proposed a sequel entitled *The Penitent*.

8. Oratorios and old age

On his return to London after the Dublin visit, Handel agreed with Rich to perform oratorios at Covent Garden in Lent, and at once set about revising and expanding *Samson* for the singers available at the theatre, who included a second tenor and two extra sopranos. He completed this work on 12 October, and on 5 February 1743 added a new organ concerto (op.7 no.2). The first performance was on 18 February with an English cast (apart from Avoglio) including Beard, Lowe, Savage, Reinhold, Mrs Cibber and Mrs Clive. Despite the opposition of the opera party, of whom Horace Walpole was voluble in his contempt for the singers, the oratorio captured the public, enjoying eight performances before the end of March. The event was important on many accounts: it established the pattern for all Handel's future work, demonstrated the capacity of English singers, with a tenor (Beard) in the leading part, to hold an audience, and split London music lovers into two camps. While Handel's course did not always run smoothly, he now had the increasingly prosperous middle class on his side, whereas most of the aristocracy supported opera in the more modern style of Galuppi, Lampugnani and their contemporaries. There were however disadvantages, as Handel soon discovered. The taste of the middle class was strongly inclined towards Evangelicalism, Methodism and a Puritan suspicion of the hedonistic element in art. It regarded the theatre as a haunt of sin and moral laxity, liable to contaminate anyone or anything with which it came in contact.

When, on 23 March, Handel gave the first London performance of *Messiah*, he advertised it without title as 'a New Sacred Oratorio', to avoid giving offence. The expedient failed. Even before the performance there was an attempt in the press to damn the enterprise as blasphemous, since an oratorio was 'an Act of Religion' unsuited to the playhouse. The work fell flat, and never took with London audiences until Handel began to perform it for charity in the Foundling Hospital Chapel in 1750.

Handel was also under fire from Jennens, who had hoped he would devote a year to the composition of *Messiah* and repeatedly expressed his disappointment

4. Title-page of the word-book for the first London performance of 'Messiah' at the Theatre Royal, Covent Garden, 1743

with the music (he preferred that of *Samson*, though contemptuous of Hamilton's libretto). In April Handel had a second stroke, and Jennens was reproached by Edward Holdsworth for contributing to it. The illness was not serious (though it may have caused a quarrel with the faithful Smith, who wrote on 28 July that 'it seems he has taken an aversion to see me'), and the friendship of the collaborators was restored by the following year; according to Jennens Handel did in fact make changes in *Messiah* at his instance. About the same time pressure was brought to bear on Handel, by the Prince of Wales among others, to compose operas for the King's Theatre. He was offered 1000 guineas for two new works, and 100 guineas to refurbish an old one (*Alessandro* was revived on 15 November under the title of *Rossane*; it is not known if Handel made the adaptation, but he certainly lent his performing score). He preferred to follow his more recent course, though in a new direction. Between 3 June and 4 July he composed *Semele*, on a text adapted, probably by Hamilton, from Congreve's libretto set by John Eccles in 1706. The extraordinary freshness and inventive genius of the music is a tribute to Handel's powers of recuperation. He followed it with three pedestrian works, the Dettingen *Te Deum* and anthem (the former full of borrowings from Urio) and another oratorio, *Joseph and his Brethren*, on a feeble text by James Miller, completed probably in September. The Dettingen music, after at least three public rehearsals, was performed at the Chapel Royal on 27 November; the *Te Deum* soon ousted the Utrecht setting in public esteem.

In Lent 1744 Handel gave another successful subscription series at Covent Garden, opening on 10 February with *The Story of Semele* (his own title),

performed 'after the Manner of an Oratorio' – though
Jennens in private called it 'a bawdy opera'. Francesina
won much applause in the title role, and according to
Mrs Delany 'the house [was] full but not crowded'. She
added that *Semele* 'has a strong party against it, viz. the
fine ladies, petit maîtres, and *ignoramus*'s. All the opera
people are enraged at Handel' – no doubt for stealing
their clothes and presenting an opera as an oratorio.
Walsh promptly published the score, without recitatives
or choruses, as he had done with *Samson* (but not
Messiah) and was to do with all subsequent works of
oratorio type. *Joseph* followed on 2 March (after rehearsals at which Handel was 'mightily out of humour' with
the singers), and then revivals of *Samson* and *Saul*. Mrs
Delany remarked that 'the oratorios fill very well, not
withstanding the spite of the opera party'. The latter
were soon to have their revenge.

For the 1744–5 season Handel took the King's
Theatre, vacated by the opera company, and planned a
much more ambitious programme, with Francesina and
an English cast, including (as usual) the Children of the
Chapel Royal under their master Bernard Gates and
some of the best voices from the church choirs. During
the summer and autumn he composed, with a single
day's interval, two of his largest and greatest works, the
musical drama *Hercules* (between 19 July and 21
August), to a libretto by Thomas Broughton based on
the *Trachiniae* of Sophocles, and the oratorio
Belshazzar (between 23 August and 23 October). Jennens, now reconciled, had supplied the text of this;
Handel's five letters to him during the summer and
autumn offer a rare glimpse of the composer at work
(see fig.5). They show him warmly engaged ('Your most
excellent Oratorio has given me great Delight in setting

5. Autograph letter (2 Oct 1744) from Handel to Charles Jennens concerning the oratorio 'Belshazzar'

it to Musick. . . . It is indeed a Noble Piece, very grand
and uncommon'), contain observations about cuts and
the insertion of anthems, and prove that he began to
compose the first two acts before receiving the words of
the third. He announced a subscription series of 24
nights and opened on 3 November with *Deborah*, which
was given twice. The season seems to have gone badly
from the start. Two performances of *Semele*, with five
inserted opera arias in Italian (perhaps an appeal to the
regular King's Theatre audience), followed in December,
and then another gap before *Hercules* ('a new Musical
Drama') on 5 January 1745, repeated on 12 January.
The reception was frigid. Mrs Cibber was ill and unable
to sing the part of Lichas, specially written for her, and
the audience so sparse that Handel was forced to
suspend the series. In a dignified letter to the *Daily
Advertiser* (17 January) he offered to refund three-
quarters of the money subscribed for season tickets.
Some of his supporters refused to take advantage of this,
and on 25 January he wrote again, promising, 'though I
am not able to fulfil the whole of my Engagement . . .
to perform what Part of it I can'. The resumption was
more than once postponed, but the series began again on
1 March with revivals of *Samson*, *Saul* and *Joseph*
and, on 27 March, the first performance of *Belshazzar*.
Again ill-luck supervened. Mrs Cibber (Daniel) was still
unable to sing, and the cast had to be shuffled at the last
minute; her music was transposed for Miss Robinson,
the tenor Beard sang much of Gobrias's part as well as
Belshazzar's, and the bass Reinhold some of Cyrus's. Not
surprisingly the reception was cool. But it is clear that
the opera audience did not relish oratorio. Elizabeth
Carter wrote that 'Handel, once so crowded, plays to
empty walls in that opera house, where there used to be

a constant *audience* as long as there were any dancers to be *seen*'. The season ended on 23 April with the 'Sacred Oratorio'; Handel had given 16 of the promised 24 performances. He never again conducted oratorios in the opera house (all his subsequent seasons were at Covent Garden, and confined to Lent), and he abandoned the subscription system in his next full season.

In the early summer he visited the Earl of Gainsborough's seat at Exton in Rutland 'for Quiet and Retirement', but was prevailed upon to set three airs with chorus to supplement a private performance of Arne's *Comus*. The score was 'intermix'd ... with several of his former Compositions' (possibly excerpts from *L'Allegro*), and the entertainment ended with fireworks in the garden. Such occasions may have been commoner than is known (the composite *Comus* was twice repeated at Exton in July 1748). Handel went on to Scarborough, and was expected to visit the Harris family at Salisbury and the Earl of Shaftesbury at Wimborne St Giles. In his later years he seems to have paid many summer visits to the country seats of his aristocratic friends, as well as to the spas at Bath, Cheltenham and Tunbridge Wells, where Smith was his regular companion.

His health continued to trouble him throughout 1745. When William Harris met him in a London street in August 'he talked much of his precarious state of health, yet he looks well enough'. Shaftesbury wrote on 24 October: 'Poor Handel looks something better. I hope he will entirely recover in due time, though he has been a good deal disordered in his head'. The landing of Charles Stuart in July and the advance of his army to Derby, which caused much alarm in the south, may have discouraged Handel from composing, though he contributed a patriotic song 'for the Gentlemen Volunteers of the City of London', sung at Drury Lane on 14 November. Early in 1746 he hurriedly put together 'a New Occasional Oratorio' from *Israel in Egypt*, *Athalia*, the coronation anthems, *Comus* and other works, with some new music; the words were compiled by Newburgh Hamilton from Milton, Spenser and the Bible. This had the first of three performances on 14 February, with a scratch orchestra led by De Fesch; Handel offered free admission to his subscribers of the previous season. During this winter and spring Gluck had two operas produced at the King's Theatre and met Handel (music by both was performed at a Musicians' Fund benefit concert on 25 March). Handel is said to have told him that he took too much trouble ('What the English like is something they can beat time to'), and to have remarked that Gluck 'knows no more of contrapunto as mein cook, Waltz'.

The victory at Culloden on 16 April inspired Handel's next oratorio, *Judas Maccabaeus*, composed during July and August. He applied, on the recommendation of the Prince of Wales, to a new librettist, the Rev. Thomas Morell, who later wrote an interesting account of his collaboration with Handel. The work 'was designed as a compliment to the Duke of Cumberland, upon his returning victorious from Scotland'. Its first performance on 1 April 1747 was an instant success, and although one of the more superficial of the oratorios it became the most popular of all during Handel's life. He constantly altered and expanded it; several pieces printed in all modern scores, including the duet and chorus 'Sion now her head shall raise', the air 'Wise men flattering' and the chorus 'See, the conquering hero comes', belong more properly to other works.

From this 1747 season Handel settled into a regular and prosperous routine, giving about 12 oratorio performances each year during Lent, generally of revivals but with occasional new compositions. His singers, most of whom stayed several years, were partly English and partly Italians from the King's Theatre, not international virtuosos but young artists whom Handel trained for their roles in English oratorio. They included the soprano Giulia Frasi, the mezzo-soprano Caterina Galli and the alto castrato Guadagni, Gluck's future Orpheus, who sang for Handel between 1750 and 1755.

In January 1747 Shaftesbury's son reported Handel as 'now in perfect health and I really think grown young again', and 'delighted' at the prospective failure of 'a most absurd and ridiculous opera going forward at present'. Nevertheless his relations with the King's Theatre must have been happier, for a Handel pasticcio, *Lucio Vero*, was staged there with great success on 14 November 1747 and followed three months later by a revival of *Rossane*. In summer 1747, and again in 1748, Handel gave evidence of renewed strength by composing two oratorios: *Alexander Balus* (1 June–4 July) and *Joshua* (19 July–19 August) in the former year, *Solomon* (5 May–13 June) and *Susanna* (11 July–24 August) in the latter. The librettist of the last two is unknown: it was certainly not Morell, who was otherwise Handel's regular collaborator from 1746. *Joshua* was introduced on 9 March 1748, *Alexander Balus* on 23 March, each with a new concerto; the elaborate scoring of these works and *Solomon* is an index of Handel's prosperity. In January 1749, according to Shaftesbury's son, 'the old Buck is excessively healthy and full of spirits'. *Susanna* was performed on 10 February, *Solomon* on 17 March. At the former Lady

Shaftesbury thought she had never seen a fuller house, but was afraid it would 'not insinuate itself so much into my approbation as most of Handel's performances do, as it is in the light *operatic* style'. For that reason it suffered an unmerited eclipse for nearly two centuries.

Two other significant events occurred that spring. Handel was commissioned to write music for a display of fireworks in Green Park to celebrate the Treaty of Aix-la-Chapelle (see fig.6). The king asked for as many martial instruments as possible and 'hoped there would be no fidles'. Handel was at first recalcitrant over this, and over a proposed public rehearsal in Vauxhall Gardens, but gave in on both issues. The rehearsal took

The GRAND WHIM for POSTERITY to Laugh at:
Being the Night View of the ROYAL FIREWORKS, as Exhibited in the Green Park, St. James's, with the Right Wing on Fire, and the cutting away the two Middle Arches to prevent the whole Fabrick from being Destroy'd. 1749

6. Engraving showing the fireworks display in Green Park, which was accompanied by a performance of the Music for the Royal Fireworks, in celebration of the Treaty of Aix-la-Chapelle, 1749

place (without fireworks) on 21 April, when the audience of 12,000 stopped the traffic for three hours; the performance, on a stage specially built by the theatrical designer Servandoni, followed six days later. The fireworks went awry, but the music was a great success. On 27 May Handel conducted a special concert for the benefit of the Foundling Hospital in its new chapel, which was still incomplete (it was not officially opened until 16 April 1753). The programme included the Music for the Royal Fireworks and two anthems, one for the Foundling Hospital, one on the Peace; the first was mostly, the second entirely a pasticcio. That summer (28 June–31 July) Handel composed the oratorio *Theodora*, and in the winter (27 December–8 January) incidental music to a play by Smollett, *Alceste*. This was commissioned by Rich for Covent Garden, along with elaborate sets by Servandoni, but for some reason never performed.

In February 1750 Shaftesbury thought he had never seen Handel 'so cool and well. He is quite easy in his behaviour, and has been pleasing himself in the purchase of several fine pictures, particularly a large Rembrandt, which is indeed excellent'. They apparently cost him about £8000. The oratorios however were less successful than usual, partly on account of earthquake shocks that kept some of the audience at home and drove others into the country. Nor was *Theodora*, first performed on 16 March with a new organ concerto (op.7 no.5) and Guadagni as Didymus (Handel's last castrato part), much to their taste; the Christian subject and tragic end may have been against it. According to Shaftesbury 'the Town don't like it at all', and Morell said that the second performance was 'very thin indeed'. Nevertheless it was the composer's favourite, and several anecdotes are told of his acerbic reactions. On 1 May he inaugurated a new organ he had presented to the Foundling Hospital with a performance of *Messiah*; this was repeated on 15 May and at least once in every subsequent year of his life. Each performance brought the hospital a net profit of about £600. During Handel's blindness they were conducted by the younger Smith, organist at the hospital from 1754, who also assisted with the Covent Garden oratorios. On three occasions the hospital accounts give precise details of the singers and instrumentalists taking part (33–8 players, five or six soloists and a chorus of 17–19, including six boys); Smith, Gates and Beard, as well as Handel, took no fee. Handel was elected a governor of the hospital on 9 May 1750. On 1 June he made his will, subsequently modified by four codicils.

His only composition that summer (28 June–5 July) was the one-act 'Interlude' *The Choice of Hercules*, based largely on the *Alceste* music. Early in August he left England for his last visit to the Continent, where he may have spent several months with his relations at and near Halle. Nothing is known of this visit except that he was injured in a coach accident between The Hague and Haarlem. In December (and again later) he was in correspondence with Telemann, an enthusiastic botanist, to whom he sent at least one crate of English plants. On 16 February 1751 Shaftesbury reported him 'actually better in health and in a higher flow of genius than he has been for several years past. His late journey has help'd his constitution vastly'. In one respect this was too rosy a picture. On 21 January Handel had begun his last oratorio, *Jephtha*, but three days before Shaftesbury's letter he was forced to break off owing to weakening of the sight of his left eye. He recorded this fact in the autograph, significantly in the middle of the chorus 'How dark, O Lord, are thy decrees', in the profound

7. Autograph MS of the middle of the chorus 'How dark, O Lord, are thy decrees' from Handel's oratorio 'Jephtha', composed 1751

anguish of which it is difficult not to see a personal reference (see fig.7). Feeling a little better, he resumed work on 23 February, his 66th birthday; but the writing bears sad witness to his disability. The oratorio was not finished until 30 August; no other composition took him so long.

The Choice of Hercules had its first performance on 1 March as 'an Additional New Act' to *Alexander's Feast* (with which it has no organic connection), together with the organ concerto in B♭ (op.7 no.3), composed during the first three days of the year. The oratorio season closed prematurely on 20 March owing to the death of the Prince of Wales. On 28 March Shaftesbury wrote that 'the Buck is now so well' as to hold out hopes of another season of renewed vigour; but he seems already to have lost the sight of one eye. In June he and Smith visited Bath and Cheltenham for the waters. On his return he was treated by Samuel Sharp, eye surgeon to Guy's Hospital, and later by two others: William Bromfield, who operated, perhaps for cataract, on 3 November 1752, and John Taylor. It is difficult to be certain of the exact nature and course of Handel's affliction; Sharp diagnosed incipient glaucoma. The *General Advertiser* of 17 August 1752 reported that he 'was seized a few Days ago with a Paralytick Disorder in his Head, which has deprived him of Sight'. Bromfield's operation brought some temporary benefit, but it did not last; according to a London paper of 27 January 1753 he had 'quite lost his sight'. The well-known letter in which Lady Shaftesbury wrote that 'it was such a melancholy pleasure, as drew tears of sorrow to see the great though unhappy Handel, dejected, wan, and dark, sitting by, not playing on the harpsichord, and to think how his light had been spent by *being overplied in music's cause'*, which has been dated 1745 and 1751, unquestionably belongs to 1753. He continued to play organ concertos from memory and later to improvise; on 3 April Shaftesbury thought his playing 'beyond what even He ever did'. According to Burney he was 'always much disturbed and agitated' by Beard's singing of Samson's air 'Total eclipse', which is said to have moved audiences to tears. The last notes known to have been written by Handel's pen were some corrections in a quintet added to *Jephtha* (first performed on 26 February 1752) for the revival of March 1753. He probably lent material for the production of *Admeto* at the King's Theatre on 12 March 1754 (this is the only opera after the Hamburg period of which both autograph and performing score are lost), but he did not arrange it.

In the same year a proposed application to parliament by the governors of the Foundling Hospital for exclusive rights in *Messiah*, other than Handel's own performances, drew an indignant repudiation from the composer; but in a codicil of 1759 he left the hospital a copy of the score and parts. During the next two seasons the Italian opera regained some of its lost ground. On 3 March 1755 Mrs Delany wrote that 'the oratorio was miserably thin', and according to Catherine Talbot (13 April 1756) the two *Messiah* nights 'made amends for the solitude of his other oratorios'. *Israel in Egypt*, revived in 1756 for the first time since 1740, 'did not take, it is too solemn for common ears' (Mrs Delany). On 8 February 1757 Shaftesbury considered that Handel 'is better than he has been for some years, and finds he can compose Chorus's as well as other music to his own . . . satisfaction. His memory is strengthened of late to an astonishing degree'. This probably refers, not to the English version of *The Triumph of Time and Truth* (first performed on 11 March that year), which contains almost no new music and for which Morell was required to dub a translation of the original Italian, but to the duet and chorus 'Sion now her head shall raise', added to *Esther* on 25 February. Shaftesbury wrote again, on 31 December, that Handel 'is pretty well and has just finished the composing of several new songs' for Cassandra Frederick. The most important was 'Wise men flattering' for *Belshazzar*, said to have been dictated, like the other late compositions, to the younger Smith. Several oratorios in the 1758 and 1759 seasons were announced as 'with new Additions and Alterations', but most of these involved no more than the transference of music from one work to another, sometimes with the words changed.

In August and September 1758 Handel was at Tunbridge Wells with Morell. His last season began on 2 March 1759 with revivals (sadly mutilated) of *Solomon* and *Susanna* and ended on 6 April with *Messiah*. His health was rapidly failing (it was only with great difficulty that he attended the oratorios), and he proposed to leave for Bath on 7 April; but he was too weak to make the journey, and took to his bed. On 11 April he dictated the fourth and final codicil to his will, in which, besides many additional bequests, he expressed a hope 'to have the permission of the Dean and Chapter of Westminster to be buried in Westminster Abbey in a private manner'. He is said to have been reconciled on his deathbed to the elder Smith, with whom he had quarrelled; but he never cut him out of his will. He died at his house in Brook Street at 8 a.m. on Saturday 14 April. The dean and chapter granted his request, and he was buried on 20 April in the south

transept of the Abbey – not privately, but in the
presence of some 3000 people. A monument by
Roubiliac, for which Handel in the last codicil provided
a 'sum not Exceeding Six Hundred Pounds', was unveiled
on 10 July 1762 and still stands (see fig.12 below).
Handel left nearly £20,000, including £1952 earned by
his oratorios in the last season. His residuary heir
was a niece in Germany. Legacies, amounting to over
£9000, made generous provision for his servants,
relations, charities and many friends, including his
librettists Morell, Hamilton and Jennens (who received
two pictures) and the violinist Dubourg. He left his
organ at Covent Garden (subsequently destroyed by
fire) to Rich, and his large harpsichord, small portative
organ, 'Musick Books' and £2000 to the elder Smith. The
'Musick Books', comprising the autographs and performing scores of nearly all his compositions, passed in due
course to the younger Smith, who in 1772 presented the
autographs to George III in return for a pension of
£200. They are now in the British Library, by far the
largest collection of any great composer's autographs
preserved in a single place. A smaller collection,
consisting mostly of fragments and sketches, was
acquired, possibly from Smith, by Lord Fitzwilliam
and is now in the Fitzwilliam Museum, Cambridge.
The performing scores are in the Staats- und
Universitätsbibliothek, Hamburg.

9. Character and personality

Hawkins, Burney, Morell, Jennens and others who knew Handel in later life left an almost unanimous verdict on his character. Hawkins described his appearance thus:

He was in his person a large made and very portly man. His gait, which was ever sauntering, was rather ungraceful, as it had in it something of that rocking motion, which distinguishes those whose legs are bowed. His features were finely marked, and the general cast of his countenance placid, bespeaking dignity attempered with benevolence, and every quality of the heart that has a tendency to beget confidence and insure esteem.

Burney, who saw fire as well as dignity in his face, added:

He was impetuous, rough, and peremptory in his manners and conversation, but totally devoid of ill-nature or malevolence; indeed, there was an original humour and pleasantry in his most lively sallies of anger or impatience, which, with his broken English, were extremely risible. His natural propensity to wit and humour, and happy method of relating common occurrences, in an uncommon way, enabled him to throw persons and things into very ridiculous attitudes. . . . Handel's general look was somewhat heavy and sour; but when he *did* smile, it was his sire the sun, bursting out of a black cloud. There was a sudden flash of intelligence, wit, and good humour, beaming in his countenance, which I hardly ever saw in any other.

The many portraits and busts, by Hudson (fig.8), Denner, Roubiliac (fig.12) and others, catch the dignity of the man, but not the humour and vitality described by Burney. Hawkins thought few of them did justice to Handel, finding the features too prominent in the Houbraken print of 1738 and 'a harshness of aspect to which his countenance was a stranger' in the mezzotint after Hudson. The Roubiliac monument in Westminster Abbey he considered 'the most perfect resemblance . . . in that the true lineaments of his face are apparent'.

Mattheson's reminiscences leave no doubt that the young Handel was a convivial companion. In Italy, at continental courts and during his early years in London he moved much in society, mixing easily with men of letters and noble and royal families, to whom his behaviour was less servile than that of most 18th-century musicians. He conducted many private concerts at the houses of Lord Burlington and the Duke of Rutland and at the Queen's Library in Green Park, where the nobility and the royal family, especially his pupil the Princess Royal, often performed. Mrs Delany's letters contain charming descriptions of parties at which Handel played to his friends. In later years he 'gradually withdrew into a state of privacy and retirement' (Hawkins), making few new friends but retaining the firm allegiance of the old, notably the Shaftesbury, Granville and Harris families. A hard worker, he came to have less and less patience with the trivialities of social life. He took no part in politics or controversy, even over his art. In his last years he was seldom seen in public, except in church, at his own oratorios and on visits to the royal family; he never kept his own carriage. He had a reputation for absolute integrity in money matters; he paid his singers and orchestra well (they were content to leave the country with promissory notes, which were always honoured) and was exceptionally generous, especially to charities. No aspersions were ever cast on his morals. He never married, and all that is known of his sex life is a remark, attributed to George III, in a copy of Mainwaring's biography: he 'scorned the advice of any but the Woman he loved, but his Amours were rather of short duration, always within the pale of his own profession'. While he was a devout Christian, his piety partook little of that milk-and-water quality attributed to him in anecdotes of the later 18th and 19th centuries. It was not incompatible with a habit of profuse swearing (in several languages) or with other pleasures of the flesh. His appetite for food and drink was notorious, and the subject of a cruel caricature by Goupy, previously a close friend. His religious attendances grew more assiduous during the years of his blindness, when Hawkins often saw him at his parish church of St George's, Hanover Square, 'on his knees, expressing by his looks and gesticulations the utmost fervour of devotion'. Handel remained a Lutheran, but totally free from bigotry: 'he would often speak of it as one of the great felicities of his life that he was settled in a country where no man suffers any molestation or inconvenience on account of his religious principles'.

Handel's imperious manner sometimes made enemies, especially among singers; the obverse of his courage and resilience was a stubbornness that did not easily brook opposition. Burney wrote of the quarrel with the Opera of the Nobility: 'If Handel's temper had at all resembled his finger, in flexibility, a reconciliation might have been effected on no very mortifying or dishonourable terms'. But if he was quick to anger ('a circumstance very terrific to a young musician', as Burney remarked when he was once the victim), he was equally quick to admit himself in the wrong. The same witness, who played in his orchestra in 1745, described the conduct of rehearsals at his Brook Street home or that of the Prince of Wales at Carlton House: 'He was a blunt and peremptory disciplinarian on these occasions, but had a humour and wit in delivering his instructions, and even in chiding and finding fault, that was peculiar to himself, and extremely diverting to all but those on whom his lash was laid'. These did not exclude persons in high places; yet the Prince and Princess of Wales received the explosions with tolerance and even with an apology.

Few great composers have been so richly endowed with humour. This could be deduced from his works, the oratorios no less than the operas; it is attested by many reported utterances, some of them told against himself. Dr Quin, who met him in Dublin, said that Handel

with his other excellences, was possessed of a great stock of humour; no man ever told a story with more. But it was requisite for the hearer to have a competent knowledge of at least four languages: English, French, Italian, and German; for in his narratives he made use of them all.

Burney thought that 'had he been as great a master of the English language as Swift, his *bons mots* would have been as frequent, and somewhat of the same kind'. (His awkward English, largely a matter of accent, is often overemphasized; he set the language beautifully in his later years, and in his letters wrote it idiosyncratically but with considerable force, whereas his German was insecure by 1731.) The exclamation 'You are welcome home, Mr Dubourg!' ('loud enough to be heard in the most remote parts of the theatre'), with which he greeted the conclusion of a long and rambling cadenza by the violinist, is justly famous. The failure of *Theodora* in 1750 elicited a number of memorable sallies: 'Never mind; the music will sound the better' (when friends commiserated with him on an empty house), 'He is a fool; the Jews will not come to it because it is a Christian story; and the Ladies will not come, because it is a virtuous one' (when another friend offered to take all the boxes if he would give it again), and (to Morell of the

third and last performance) 'Will you be there next
Friday night, and I will play it to you?'.

Handel had neither false pride nor false modesty; he
knew his own value, and was capable of stern self-
criticism. He ranked the chorus 'He saw the lovely
youth' in *Theodora* 'far beyond' the *Messiah* Hallelujah,
and told Hawkins that 'Cara sposa' in *Rinaldo* and
'Ombra cara' in *Radamisto* were the finest arias he ever
composed; but when a friend remarked on the wretched
music they were hearing in Vauxhall Gardens, he
replied: 'You are right, sir, it is very poor stuff; I
thought so myself when I wrote it'. He was affronted
when the bishops sent him words to set for the coronation anthems, preferring to rely on his own knowledge
of the Bible and choose for himself. He thought little of
some of his more popular works, including *Judas
Maccabaeus*, and called Cardinal Pamphili, author of
the text of *Il trionfo del Tempo* and a cantata comparing
Handel favourably with Orpheus, 'an old Fool!'. When
Jennens asked 'Why Fool? because he wrote an
Oratorio? perhaps you would call *me* fool for the same
reason!', Handel replied: 'So I would, if you flatter'd me,
as He did'.

His relations with other composers were never close,
except in his youth, and even then a sturdy independence is apparent. He maintained his friendship with
Telemann, though they seldom met, but grew weary of
the importunities of Mattheson. He disliked Greene and
despised the pedantry of Pepusch (who in return
abstained from the general chorus of Handel's praise
and called him 'a good *practical* musician'), but rever-
enced some of his predecessors. Hawkins recalled that
he always spoke of Rameau 'in terms of great respect'.
His opinion of Purcell emerges from a revealing anec-

8. *Handel: portrait (1756) by Thomas Hudson*

dote recorded by R. J. S. Stevens in 1775:

When Handel was blind, and attending a performance of the Oratorio of *Jephtha*, Mr [William] Savage, my master, who sat next him, said, 'This movement, sir, reminds me of some of old Purcell's music'. 'O got te teffel', said Handel, 'if Purcell had lived, he would have composed better music than this.'

Handel's fame as a keyboard player spread early throughout Europe, and he remained a virtuoso to the last. Festing and Arne heard him play the organ at Oxford in 1733 and told Burney 'that neither themselves, nor any one else of their acquaintance, had ever before heard such extempore, or such premeditated playing, on that or any other instrument'. His improvisations, according to Hawkins, 'stole on the ear in a slow and solemn progression; the harmony close wrought, and as full as could possibly be expressed; the passages concatenated with stupendous art, the whole at the same time being perfectly intelligible, and carrying the appearance of great simplicity'. Burney described his touch on the harpsichord as 'so smooth, and the tone of the instrument so much cherished, that his fingers seemed to grow to the keys. They were so curved and compact, when he played, that no motion, and scarcely the fingers themselves, could be discovered'. Although he early gave up practising the violin, years later 'his manner of touching it was such as the ablest masters would have been glad to imitate'. Hawkins, whose testimony that is, added that 'without a voice he was an excellent singer of such music as required more of the pathos of melody than a quick and voluble expression', and once at a private concert 'was prevailed on to sing a slow song, which he did in such a manner, that Farinelli, who was present, could hardly be persuaded to sing after him'.

10. Method of composition; style

Handel's habit of improvisation was linked with his composition method. He worked fast. While his careful dating of autographs indicates that nearly all his major works were committed to paper within an astonishingly short space of time (the three weeks spent on *Messiah* is the most famous of many examples), he undoubtedly worked out ideas in advance, both in his head and in sketches; a number of the latter survive, and they sometimes show a single idea subjected to repeated polishing almost in the manner of Beethoven. The autographs themselves often continue the process; but the initial impulse came from his fingers on the keyboard, or the aural associations of verbal imagery, or both together. Morell left a revealing account of Handel at work on *Judas Maccabaeus*. As soon as the librettist suggested the text of the chorus 'Fall'n is the foe' he sat down at the harpsichord and began to improvise on a theme clearly suggested by the image in the words, 'and immediately carried on the composition as we have it in that most admirable chorus'. A year later, when Morell gave him the words of Cleopatra's air 'Convey me to some peaceful shore' in *Alexander Balus*, he cried out '*Damn* your Iambics!'. Morell offered to change them to trochees and went into the next room to do so, only to find about three minutes later that Handel had set them as they stood.

The existence of many movements, especially in instrumental works, that begin with the same germ motif and then diverge, often in unexpected directions, is

evidence of a technique based on improvisation. Linked
with this is Handel's well-known habit of borrowing, on
which much ink has been spilt and much moral indigna-
tion generated. It is on the face of it surprising that a
composer with such prodigious powers of invention
should have needed to borrow at all; but Handel's
capacity for development and contrapuntal combination
was equally if not more remarkable. By temper an op-
portunist, he used anything that came to hand – chiefly
his own earlier works, but those of others when he found
it convenient. Many composers did the same, if to a
lesser degree; no stigma was attached, provided (in
Mattheson's metaphor) the borrower repaid the loan
with interest by developing what he took and making it
his own. Handel did not always do that. In the mid-
1730s he began to incorporate entire movements by
other composers into his major works. *Israel in Egypt*
affords the most prominent example. Dent plausibly
linked these wholesale borrowings with Handel's mental
and physical breakdown at this period, and suggested
that his powers of invention may have been temporarily
sapped. The moral issue would loom large only if his
reputation could be shown to depend on what he took
from others, which is manifestly not the case. Far more
common than the wholesale borrowings are his transformation of another man's work, by a process of grouting,
into a specifically Handelian composition, and the
abstraction of a theme or melodic germ which is then
used as a basis for a fresh start – or improvisation. He
made no attempt to conceal his borrowings, which he
several times took from printed works while their
authors were alive (a conspicuous creditor was his
friend Telemann, to whose *Musique de table* he subscribed publicly in 1733). His habit was well known to

his contemporaries, at least six of whom mentioned it
during his life: Mattheson in 1722 and 1740, Prévost in
1733, Scheibe in 1745 (these three in print), F. M.
Veracini in an unpublished treatise, Jennens in a letter of
1743 and William Mason in a letter of 1755. Further
borrowings are still being discovered; one of the most
interesting is the use in *Serse* of Giovanni Bononcini's
setting of the same libretto. Here both the grouting and
the improvisatory methods are repeatedly illustrated,
not least in Handel's most famous melody, 'Ombra mai
fù'. There could be no clearer illustration of a borrower
repaying his debt with compound interest.

Handel's mature style is empirical and eclectic.
His creative personality was so strong that he was
able to assimilate what he wanted from whatever tradition he met, without awkwardness or incongruity, and to
comprehend the new without abandoning the old. While
German, Italian, French and English elements can be
easily detected – the first three as early as his Hamburg
years – the central core was Italian. The most characteristic German form of the period, the chorale, left occasional traces in the Chandos anthems and a few
oratorio choruses, but it is far less prominent, even in
the *Brockes Passion*, than in the music of his German
contemporaries. In orchestration, especially the free
treatment of woodwind instruments, and the use of
sharply rhythmic accompaniment figures to generate
tension, he learnt much from Keiser, whose melodic
idiom, though individual, was short-breathed. The best
of his ideas want space to develop their full potential;
that is precisely what Handel gave them when he borrowed from *Octavia*, first in Italy and later in London.

Handel's debt to Italy was not confined to the music
of a single period or style. While Alessandro Scarlatti in

vocal works and Corelli in instrumental were the domin-
ant influences, the earlier Venetian composers from
Cavalli onwards lie behind some movements, not only in
the Venice opera *Agrippina* but as late as *Serse*, in
which Handel, parting company with the da capo in half
the arias, employed arioso forms that would scarcely
have been out of place in Cavalli's original setting of
Minato's libretto in 1654. When, after Handel settled in
England, the idiom of Italian opera was transformed by
Vinci, Leo, Pergolesi and their contemporaries from a
polyphonic to a homophonic style based on soaring
vocal lines over steady basses and chordal accompaniments, Handel simply added the new method to his
repertory. There are instances as early as *Ottone* ('Dopo
l'orrore'), and many more in the operas composed after
his visit to Italy in 1729; but it never ousted the rich and
fertile polyphony that was already obsolete elsewhere.
Besides using Purcell's ceremonial works as a model for
his first settings of English words, Handel must have
heard a great deal of his dramatic music in the London
theatres, where it was constantly revived. Purcellian
turns of melody and harmony, including false relations
at cadences, are present intermittently in many settings
of English words from *Acis and Galatea* to *Semele* and
Theodora. The vast range of the oratorio choruses, from
recitative to double fugue, from a dramatic ejaculation
to a mighty cataract of sound in several movements, can
be seen as a personal fusion – and extension – of every
European tradition that Handel had encountered in the
course of a long life.

A distinctive feature of all his music, instrumental,
vocal or mixed, is his infallible ear for texture. No
composer has obtained such variety of colour from a
string orchestra as Handel in the Grand Concertos of

op.6, or such overwhelming splendour as in the coronation anthems. His range of instrumentation in the operas
and oratorios is very wide, but depends as much on
finesse as on mass. The air with continuo only is used
with marvellous aptness as late as *Semele*, to suggest the
intimacy of the heroine's invocations to sleep. The 1718
score of *Acis and Galatea* is a masterpiece of economy;
that of *Saul* with its carillon, three trombones, double-
bass kettledrums and two organs has few contemporary
rivals for grandeur and sonority. For oriental subjects
Handel used exotic or unusual groups, four horns, harp,
theorbo and a written-out part for viola da gamba in
Giulio Cesare, mandolin and harp in *Alexander Balus*.
The criteria are aptness to the subject, clarity and an
instinctive knowledge of what will work in performance.
Complication for its own sake he eschewed. In writing
for solo voice he studied each artist's peculiar qualities
so closely that it is often possible, on the basis of the
music, to assign unattributed airs to the singers for
whom they were written. In his operas, where convention required the heroic male parts to be taken by high
voices, he showed a strong preference for the alto register, using women when castratos were not available –
and sometimes when they were. It follows from his acute
sensitivity to balance that octave transposition of
castrato roles for baritones and basses, which Handel
invariably avoided in revivals (he preferred to write new
music when he had a new voice) does grave damage to
the musical fabric. It also disturbs the characterization,
in which vocal pitch is an important element. When
Handel wrote for tenors and basses he used a different
manner and a different type of coloratura. Even when he
was writing heroic roles for the tenors Beard and Lowe
in the later oratorios he still gave important male parts

to women, some of them (Alexander Balus, Solomon, Joachim in *Susanna*) taking precedence over tenor and bass alike.

Handel was a master of the unexpected on every level; not only where a dramatic context required an element of surprise but in manifold details of line, harmony or rhythm, and especially in length of phrase. It is this that articulates and imparts energy and expression to his melodies, which are often unsymmetrical and extended longer than the ear expects. He could be plain and foursquare, especially in ceremonial works designed for large forces in public buildings or the open air, where intimate subtleties would be wasted. No composer was ever more practical in fitting his music to the place or occasion for which it was written. This empirical quality extends to his treatment of musical forms, especially the fugue and the aria. He could write strict fugues, but preferred to enlarge his territory by varying fugal texture with block harmony, unisons and other expedients. In a lesser artist the results might be lame and clumsy; Handel frequently created brilliant and novel effects by ignoring the rules or temporarily abandoning them. He wrote always for the ear, never for the eye of the score-reader or the tidy mind of the mathematician. His obbligato instrumental parts, unlike Bach's, do not compete on equal terms with the voice; they pause when it enters, in order not to cover the words or complicate the texture.

All composers of vocal music in the age of the doctrine of the Affections drew much of their musical imagery from the mood and language of the text. Handel, while no exception, was more than usually susceptible both to visual impressions (he collected pictures, frequented art galleries and had a keen eye for the beauties of nature) and to the cadences of poetry, not least poetry in English. If he occasionally misaccented a word, he often penetrated below the surface meaning, and on many occasions he set the language with a subtlety few native composers have equalled. Not even Purcell surpassed his treatment of the chorus 'May no rash intruder' in Act 1 of *Solomon*. Handel has been criticized, in his own day and since, for his realistic approach to the frogs and flies in *Israel in Egypt* and the miracle of the sun standing still in *Joshua*. He may have been satisfied with an obvious image; more frequently he seized an idea and by creative force converted it from a literal equivalent into a potent musical metaphor. The strides of Polyphemus in 'Wretched lovers' and the genuflection of the widow of Nain in *Theodora* ('Lowly the matron bowed') are translations, not copies. Perhaps the work in which this quality is most powerfully displayed is *L'Allegro, il Penseroso ed il Moderato*, especially its first two parts. Although there is no plot and no continuous thread except a contrast between two temperaments, Handel, converting to new ends the flexibility of form gained in *Athalia* and *Saul*, exploits Milton's concrete imagery to paint a series of genre pictures almost tangible in their sensuous perception, the most vivid evocation in music of the English countryside. It cannot be accidental that the finest poetry he encountered – Milton, Dryden, Congreve and a few lines of Pope – inspired some of his richest music.

Handel was by training and temperament a composer for the theatre, which monopolized his attention throughout his life, and for which all his most important works were conceived. Like Mozart he possessed in the highest degree the supreme attributes of the musical

dramatist, a profound understanding of human character together with the technique to embody it in terms of
his art and the detachment to view it in proportion. His
sympathy was Shakespearean in its range and breadth.
He scarcely ever condemned a character or presented
him or her in a wholly unfavourable light. His villains,
with few exceptions, do not finally repel sympathy, or at
least understanding. Saul's insane jealousy yields to a
noble courage at the last, and even Athalia wins respect
by her defiance of overwhelming odds. Sometimes
Handel's refusal to pass judgment subverted the ostens-
ible moral of the story and the intentions of the librettist.
The sorceresses in his magic operas, especially Melissa
in *Amadigi* and Alcina, though their motives are de-
structive of the happiness of everyone else on stage, have
their frustrated longing portrayed in music of such
intensity that they assume the stature of tragic heroines.
The ambitious and envious matriarch Gismonda in
Ottone has the redeeming quality of love for her
worthless son; the aria in which Handel expressed it is
so moving that it almost unbalances the plot. His women
are exceptionally subtle and varied. Cleopatra in *Giulio
Cesare* rivals Shakespeare's heroine in her infinite variety. Dejanira in *Hercules* is a superb portrait of a wife
whose honourable instincts are gradually eaten away by
jealousy until she kills her husband and loses her reason.
In *Semele* Handel drew perhaps the most penetrating
and explicit picture in dramatic music of a woman's
insatiable sexual appetite. His Delilah is so seductive
that we almost lose patience with Samson's stern
rejection of her proffered comfort. Yet the heroic
courage of the virgin martyr Theodora and the self-
sacrificing Iphis (in *Jephtha*), to whom life is sweet, are
quite unsullied (unlike the words Morell put in their

mouths) by any suggestion of priggishness or senti-mentality. Some situations and emotional states seldom failed to draw an overwhelming response: the sufferings of unhappy, scorned or separated lovers (a common operatic situation, but never so piercingly presented except by the few masters of comparable stature), the devotion of a father to his child (a link perhaps with Handel's childlessness), mental derangement, the mellowness of old age, the inescapable conflict between Man and destiny, between the sweetness and brevity of life and the finality of death. Behind several if not all of these situations one may suspect the spur of personal experience; but it is clear that Handel's insight into the vicissitudes of human nature was subject to no identifiable limit.

11. Keyboard and chamber music

Three keyboard collections appeared during Handel's life. The first *Suites de pieces*, printed by Cluer and issued on 14 November 1720, contains a preface in which Handel wrote: 'I have been obliged to publish some of the following Lessons, because surrepticious and incorrect Copies of them had got Abroad. I have added several new ones to make the Work more usefull'. He promised to augment these eight suites if they met with a favourable reception; and a second collection was published by Walsh in 1733, apparently taken from Roger's 'surrepticious' edition of 1719. In 1735 Walsh issued six *Fugues or Voluntarys for the Organ or Harpsichord*. Other pieces appeared singly or in groups, some of them abroad, and substantial posthumous collections, including further suites, were added by Arnold (*c*1793) and more recently (1928) from the Aylesford manuscripts.

None of these very numerous compositions can be exactly dated. According to Hawkins Handel composed the suites for his pupil Princess Anne; Burney said that 'the chief part of his hautbois concertos, sonatas, lessons, and organ fugues' was written at Cannons. Probably the bulk of Handel's keyboard music dates from before 1720; in view of his habit of re-using old material some of it may have originated in Hamburg. The six fugues (two of them later adapted for choruses in *Israel in Egypt*) stand apart from the rest; they are more formal and severe than usual with Handel, and almost devoid of decoration. With this possible exception the music was intended not for public but for

Stops

An Open Diapason — of Metal throughout to be in Front.
a Stopt Diapason — the Treble Metal and the Bass Wood.
a Principal — of Metal throughout.
a Twelfth — of Metal throughout.
a Fifteenth — of Metal throughout.
a great Tierce — of Metal throughout.
a Flute Stop — Such a one as in Freemans Organ.

I am glad of the Opportunity to show you my
attention, wishing you all Health and Happiness
I remain with great Sincerity and Respect
Sir
Your

London. Sept. 30.
1749.

most obedient and most humble
servant
George Frideric Handel

9. Part of an autograph letter (30 Sept 1749) from Handel
to Jennens containing specifications for an organ Jennens
planned to build at his home in Gopsal. This instrument can
still be seen, slightly altered, in the church of Great
Packington, Warwickshire

domestic use, including no doubt the education of the princess. Alfred Mann (1964–5) suggested that a series of autographs in the Fitzwilliam Museum represents Handel's manual of instruction. The texts of the keyboard works have a Protean fluidity; many of the same ideas were reworked at different periods, and appear not only in more than one suite but in chamber and orchestral works and dance movements in the operas. The suites vary widely in plan, number of movements and cohesiveness; some seem haphazard, others employ thematic interconnection. This can produce an effect of organic unity; elsewhere, for example in the G minor suite from the second volume, the related movements look like alternative improvisations on the same material. The preludes in particular suggest written-out improvisation. The majority of movements conform to the usual dance types of the period, generally in binary but occasionally in ternary form. Besides fugues there are a number of chaconnes and sets of variations, some of extravagant length. They are melodic and decorative rather than architectural in plan and contain little tonal contrast.

In view of Handel's aversion to system and the fact that many of the posthumous pieces are chips from the workshop floor not intended for the public eye, it is not surprising that the music is uneven in quality and often below that of Bach and Domenico Scarlatti in technical finish. The invention however often rises very high. Its vitality springs more often from melody and rhythm than from harmonic adventurousness, though there are striking exceptions in the F minor and F♯ minor suites from the first book. The part-writing is characteristically free; Handel is far less rigorous than Bach in preserving the number of voices. As usual at this period, the music would be ornamented in performance and extended by improvisation. The fact that Handel often left the texture bare, and that the music, conceived in terms of the harpsichord, transfers badly to the modern piano, has tended to give it a lower reputation than it deserves.

The sonatas for melody instruments and continuo also present problems of dating, and sometimes of authenticity. Four sets appeared during Handel's life: 12 sonatas for flute, recorder, violin or oboe with continuo (op.1) and six trio sonatas for two violins, oboes or flutes with continuo (op.2), published by Walsh about 1730 (for some reason under the imprint of Jeanne Roger of Amsterdam), three sonatas for flute and continuo by Walsh in 1730, and seven trio sonatas for violins or flutes with continuo (op.5) by Walsh in 1739. About 1732 Walsh reissued opp.1 and 2 (under his own imprint), replacing two of the op.1 sonatas by new ones: of the 15 printed by Chrysander, nos.14 and 15, in the earlier issue, were rejected in favour of nos.10 and 12. All four are for violin and of unproven authenticity. No.13, the violin sonata in D, was first printed by Chrysander and does not belong to op.1. This splendidly spacious work, which survives in autograph, is the finest of the solo sonatas. The others in op.1 have been variously assigned on internal evidence (where no autograph survives) to flute, recorder, oboe, violin and viola da gamba. Posthumous publications include an early sonata for viola da gamba with written-out keyboard part, three sonatas for recorder and continuo assembled from fragments in the Fitzwilliam Museum, and a lively trio for two clarinets and horn. Chrysander supplemented op.2 with three further trio sonatas, printed from copies in Dresden, and added a set

of six for two oboes and continuo which he dated about
1696. Handel is said to have remarked of these sonatas:
'I used to write like the Devil in those days, but chiefly
for the hautbois, which was my favourite instrument'.
But it is doubtful if they are his; and if they are, they can
scarcely be so early.

As with the keyboard music and concertos, many of
the sonatas exist in alternative versions, and the great
majority use material that occurs elsewhere, in modified
or identical form; there was a principle of interchange-
ability in Handel's instrumental works. While it is not
always possible to determine which version came first,
Handel in later life drew on the sonatas for stock, using
movements as the basis for choruses or symphonies in
Belshazzar, *Solomon*, *Jephtha* and other works. It is
likely that the op.5 set was assembled from music
already in existence. Certainly the sonatas of op.2 are
finer and more solidly composed; they belong to the
sonata da chiesa type with two pairs of movements,
slow and fast, often linked by a half-close and with a
change of mode for the second slow movement. Many of
the opp.1 and 5 sonatas are freer in form (*sonata da
camera*) with up to seven movements, sometimes ending
with a suite of dances. The music, inevitably indebted to
the tradition established by Corelli, shows Handel perfectly at ease with miniature forms and the intimate
mood and scale of the chamber sonata.

12. Music for orchestra

Most of Handel's orchestral music is a by-product of his work for the theatre. Exceptions are the Water and Fireworks Music, designed for performance in the open air. The former incorporates at least two and probably three suites composed on different occasions in different keys (F, D and G) for different groups of instruments. It is splendidly inventive and sonorous, especially the D major suite with trumpets, and deserves the popularity it has always enjoyed, even when sapped by modern rescoring. The Music for the Royal Fireworks is still grander; it is perhaps the only work of Handel that thrives on what may be called a Crystal Palace orchestra. The autograph specifies 18 brass instruments, 37 woodwind (including double bassoon) and three timpani; Handel added string parts, doubling the wind, possibly for the original performance and certainly for the Foundling Hospital one.

A number of orchestral works, including the suite-like overtures later attached to *Il pastor fido*, *Teseo*, *Silla* and *Ottone*, may date from Handel's residence in Hanover. Two of the three concertos with solo oboe and one with solo violin are also early; the other oboe concerto (Chrysander's no.2) is an arrangement of the overtures to two Chandos anthems, published by Walsh in 1740 together with a C major concerto composed in 1736 for *Alexander's Feast*. The six Concerti Grossi op.3, often miscalled 'oboe concertos', appeared in 1734; the first edition included a different, probably spurious, concerto as no.4 and only two of the five

movements of no.5. Much if not all of the music dates
from many years before; movements from nos.4 and 6
had been used in *Amadigi* (1716) and *Ottone* (1723) and
were probably not new then. The publication bears signs
of ad hoc assembly; some concertos are ill-balanced in
tonal structure or number of movements. The result,
though uneven, contains much that is strong and characteristic, and some pleasantly unpredictable scoring, with
recorders sometimes replacing the oboes and violas and
cellos divided.

Far finer are the 12 Grand Concertos for strings
op.6, which rank with Bach's Brandenburg set as one of
the twin peaks of the Baroque concerto. Nowhere is
Handel's empirical attitude to accepted forms more
triumphantly vindicated. Despite the limitation of
resources (Handel added oboe parts to four of the set,
but they were not published until modern times and
contribute little) the exceptional variety of the music
embraces texture as well as plan, mood, rhythm, part-
writing and the length of phrases and paragraphs. This
unexpectedness is so comprehensive that when Handel
did follow a pattern he almost achieved a *coup d'état* of
surprise. Hawkins, deceived perhaps by the spontaneity
and euphony of the music, condemned these concertos
as 'destitute of art and contrivance', the very qualities in
which they are pre-eminent: Handel had no superior in
the manipulation and rejuvenation of formulae. The
emotional range extends from the spaciousness and
majesty of no.1 to the tragedy of no.3, from the haunt-
ing musette-rondo of no.6 and the serenity of the E
major Larghetto of no.12 to lighthearted dances and
jocular prestidigitation with eccentric and ungainly
fugue subjects. These concertos are the apotheosis of
improvisation; every new idea or development, however

SUBSCRIBERS NAMES

HIS ROYAL HIGHNESS   THE DUKE OF CUMBERLAND

HER ROYAL HIGHNESS   THE PRINCESS OF ORANGE

HER ROYAL HIGHNESS   THE PRINCESS AMELIA

HER ROYAL HIGHNESS   THE PRINCESS CAROLINE

HER ROYAL HIGHNESS   THE PRINCESS MARY

HER ROYAL HIGHNESS   THE PRINCESS LOUISA.

A

Academy of Musick at Dublin
2 Sets

B

Willoughby Bertie Esq.
Daniel Bailey Esq.
Mr. Thoˢ Birch
Mr. Bogg

C

Right Hon. Countess of Car-
lisle
Right Hon. Earl Cowper
Right Hon. Earl Cholmondley
Rt. Hon. Lord James Cavendish
Hon. Thoˢ Carter Esq. Master
of the Rolls in Ireland

Brig. Cornwall
John Cotton Esq.
Henry Cornelison Esq.
Crown and Anchor Society
Musical Society in Canterbury
Miss Cox of Bartlets Buildings
Mr. Collier
Mr. Ham Croft
Society of Musick at the Castle
in Paternoster Row. 3 Sets
Mr. Richˢ Collet.
Mr. John Stephen Carbonell

D

General Dormer
Rev. Sr. John Dolben Bart.
Thoˢ Lee Dummer Esq.
Wm. Dobbs Esq.
Mr. Dancaff, Merchant
Mr. Dickinson

E

Mr. Ephraim Evans. 4 Sets
Mr. Christopher Ebelin

F

Wm. Freeman Esq.
Henry Furnese Esq.
Capt. Furnese
Francis Fauquier Esq.
Mr. De Fetch
Mr. Fawcet

G

Right Hon. Lord Guernsey
Hon. B. Granville Esq.
Mr. Gough. 2 Sets

SUBSCRIBERS NAMES

H

John Harrington Esq. 2 Sets
Rev. Mr. Wm. Harrington
Robert Holden Esq.
James Harris Esq.
Thoˢ Harris Esq.
Mr. James Hunter
Mr. John Hunter
Mr. John Henry. Surgeon
Mr. Hugford
Mr. Hudson

Monday Nights Musical Society
at ẏ Globe Tavern Fleetstr. 2 Sets
Mr. Marchant
Mr. Rudolph Myre
Mr. Mahoon

I

Charles Jennens Esq. 2 Sets

K

Mr. Henry Jernigan
Mrs. Ann Jones of Stepney

L

Sir Windham Knatchbull Bart.

Ladies Concert at Lincoln
Mr. Charles Lawrence

M

Rt. Hon. Lord Malpas
Edward Montague Esq.
Robert Myre Esq.
John Maxwell Esq.
Henry Moore Esq.
Mr. Moses Mendes

N

Mr. Benjamin Short
Mr. Shuttleworth

O

Mr. Henry Needler

P

Musical Society at Oxford
2 Sets

Sir Mark Playdell Bart.
Hon. Phillip Percival Esq.
Thoˢ Pitt Esq.
James Peachy Esq.
Philharmonic Society at the
Crown and Anchor. 3 Sets
Mr. Joseph Porter
Mr. John Porter

Q

R

Rt. Hon. Earl of Rockingham
John Rich Esq. 3 Sets
Mr. Robinson Organift

S

Rt. Hon. Countess Dowager of Shaftsbury
Rt. Hon. Countess of Shaftsbury

Rt. Hon. Earl of Shaftsbury 2 Sets
Hon. John Spencer Esq.
Salisbury Society of Musick
Swan Society of Musick. 2 Sets
Mr. Stone
Mr. Solinus

T

Bennet Tate Esq.
Wm. Theod Esq.
Wm. Trumbull Esq.
Mr. Jonathan Tyree. 4 Sets
Mr. Thompson M.M.

V

Mr. Verian

W

Hon. —— Witherington Esq.
Hon. Wm. Watson Esq.
Humphrey Whyrley Esq.
John Wolf Esq.
Richˢ Wingfield Esq.
Richˢ Warner Esq.
Mr. Charles Weideman

Y

Z

Mr. Zincke

10. List of subscribers to the 12 Grand Concertos, published by Walsh in 1740

11. *Autograph MS of the Adagio, and opening of the Allegro, from Handel's Organ Concerto op.4 no.2, composed 1735–6*

extraneous at first glance, is integrated by the sheer force of Handel's creative personality. The three *Concerti a due cori*, really triple concertos for string orchestra with two wind groups, date from 1747–8 and have something of the jubilant resonance of the Fireworks music, especially the third, composed for use in *Judas Maccabaeus*. The other two, based for the most part on choruses from earlier oratorios (including *Messiah*, still unfamiliar in London), were probably written for the first performances of *Joshua* and *Alexander Balus*.

The organ concerto, though faintly prefigured in a 'sonata' in the 1707 *Il trionfo del Tempo*, was invented by Handel as a supplement to his greater innovation, the English oratorio. It made its appearance in 1735, when he decided to use his own virtuosity on the keyboard between the acts to replace or reinforce that of the Italian singers. Nearly all the organ concertos can be exactly dated and linked with the oratorios for which they were intended. The first set of six (op.4) belong to 1735–6; no.6 was originally a harp concerto for Powell to play in *Alexander's Feast*. The second set, issued in 1740 without opus number, contains two concertos of 1739 and four arrangements from op.6; the third (op.7), published posthumously in 1761, was composed on various occasions between 1740 and 1751. Arnold printed two more concertos in 1797. The first three sets were described as 'for harpsichord or organ', and nearly all are equally appropriate to the former instrument. Handel played them on a small organ with very few stops; only op.7 no.1, written in 1740, requires pedals (such an instrument must have been available at the Lincoln's Inn Fields theatre), and this work contains the most substantial structure in any Handel concerto, the mighty chaconne that embraces the first two movements (in different metres). The organ concertos are inevitably less finished than the Grand Concertos of op.6, though they share the same unsystematic approach and no two are identical in plan: since Handel designed them for his own use, with opportunities for improvisation (he probably never played the same work twice in exactly the same way), the scores are full of 'ad lib' markings, sometimes applied to whole movements. The music, which has a deceptive simplicity and clarity appropriate to the chamber and the theatre rather than to the modern concert hall, loses its flavour when transferred to a large organ and an inflated orchestra. It requires a continuo harpsichord in addition to the soloist.

13. Church and vocal chamber music

In the course of his life Handel composed for three Churches, Roman Catholic (the Latin psalms), Lutheran (the *Brockes Passion*) and Anglican. Differences of style are less conspicuous than the functional quality common to all; only the *Brockes Passion* and one or two motets may not have been designed to meet a specific demand. The Anglican works were written either for a private chapel (the Chandos anthems and *Te Deum* and the Foundling Hospital anthem) or for ceremonial use in an act of state worship, when they were performed by the Chapel Royal choir and a large orchestra in Westminster Abbey or St Paul's Cathedral. This is occasional music in the literal sense: the occasions were the celebration of the Treaty of Utrecht (1713), the coronation of George II (1727), two royal weddings (1734 and 1736), the funeral of Queen Caroline (1737), the victory at Dettingen (1743) and the Peace of Aix-la-Chapelle (1748). The other Chapel Royal anthems, mostly expanded from Chandos pieces, probably celebrated the king's return from Hanover or some similar royal event. Apart from the funeral anthem, in which personal emotion penetrated the solemnity of ecclesiastical tradition, the music does not show Handel at his most profound. Such was not required and might have been intrusive. But the spaciousness, energy and architectural splendour he was able to impart to these public utterances was exactly appropriate and has never been surpassed in its kind. The use of one or more of his 1727 anthems at every subsequent British coronation

GEORGE FREDERICK HANDEL Esqr.
born February XXIII. MDCLXXXIV.
died April XIV. MDCCLIX.   L.F.Roubiliac inv.^t et sc

confirms this.

In addition to the cantatas of his Italian years, on which something has already been said (see chapter 2 above), Handel left 22 chamber duets and two trios with continuo accompaniment. These fall into three groups: a few composed in Italy before 1710, about a dozen copied in Hanover about 1711 and perhaps composed then, and seven written in London in 1741–5. The second group shows the influence of Steffani, whom Handel evidently used as a model. Why he returned to the Italian duet in the late London years has never been explained, unless he was seriously thinking of returning to the Continent. These late duets are significant because Handel used them in the choruses of *Messiah* and *Belshazzar*. They contribute not a little to the airy texture of several *Messiah* choruses, like 'For unto us'. A few of the bigger cantatas are public rather than chamber music, and two or three at least were written in London; but the great majority were designed for the drawing-rooms of Italian aristocrats, with Handel himself at the harpsichord. He used them, whether consciously or not, as a trial ground for that exploration of the human heart he was to consummate in the theatre. Though often more intimate in mood, they differ little in content and technique from many scenes in the operas, in which a good deal of their music, unchanged or modified, ultimately found a place.

12. Handel: monument by Louis François Roubiliac, unveiled on 10 July 1762, in Westminster Abbey, London

14. Operas

It is only in the last half-century that Handel's operas have been rediscovered; apart from a fragment of *Almira* reduced to one short act (1878), none was staged anywhere between 1754 and 1920. They were regarded as dead along with the *opera seria* convention to which they subscribed. It is true that Handel did not reform or break out of that convention, with its concentration on recitative and da capo aria, an occasional duet, and a happy end expressed in an ensemble or *coro*, to the extent that Gluck did. The way he made it work in the theatre could not be demonstrated until modern producers discovered how the 18th-century stage operated: it worked by exploiting its peculiarities and limitations, such as the single rise and fall of the curtain at beginning and end of the opera and the quick scene changes executed in full view of the audience, and relating them to the musical structure in such a way as to play on and defeat the listener's expectation.

In a narrowly circumscribed convention a slight deviation can achieve a disproportionate effect. By manipulating the shape of the da capo aria and in particular varying the incidence, length, texture and regularity of the ritornellos at the beginning and end of the main sections (and in the middle), and by associating such strokes with a point of drama or character, he turned the most static of forms into something potentially dynamic. The number of different designs he created by this means, with the aid of contrasts in tempo, metre, rhythm and key, is almost beyond counting; in extreme cases,

such as 'Deggio dunque' in *Radamisto*, he could deceive
the ear into thinking that da capo form had been abandoned altogether. The next step was to give a cumulative
dynamic thrust to a scene, an act and a whole opera by
so placing the arias that they build up the characters
facet by facet and at the same time draw taut the
dramatic conflict. Handel did this partly by long-term
contrasts of mood and pace and partly by tonality.
When a slow chromatic aria in the minor follows several
quick pieces in the major, perhaps with a radical change
of scoring, its impact is greatly enhanced, especially if it
occurs at the point of maximum weight at the end of an
act. Handel sometimes built a whole opera round one
tonal centre (*Imeneo*) and associated characters with
particular keys (Cleopatra, Antigone in *Admeto*); he
regularly pointed a switch of dramatic emphasis by a
shift in tonal direction. That was his almost invariable
method of marking a change of scene; the visual transformation of the sets is reflected in the music. Such a
method depends for success on a coherent and work-
manlike libretto (there is evidence that, at least in the
Royal Academy years, Handel exercised firm control
over this) and on the composer's ability to deploy an
exceptional fund of musical invention in the arias themselves. It does not take many weak links to break the
chain. Handel's greatest operas contain so few inferior
or superfluous arias that they are difficult to cut without
damage to the structure.

In some respects Handel did loosen the convention.
He carried the accompanied recitative to an elaboration
and an intensity of emotion it had never attained before
and was not to reach again until Mozart or even later. In
the remarkable episodes of Bajazet's suicide in
Tamerlano and Orlando's madness, where simple and

accompanied recitative, arioso and aria are inter-
mingled, the forward drive of the drama takes control
and dictates new musical forms. Elsewhere Handel
allowed a character to interrupt another's aria or quote
it back at him ironically in a different context. Act 1 of
Metastasio's *Poro* libretto ends with a scene in which
two estranged lovers do this simultaneously, each in a
mood of disillusionment citing the other's earlier vow of
constancy. Handel's setting works the two arias together
as an extended duet that marvellously combines irony,
deft counterpoint and lyrical beauty. Handel exploited
the conventional exit after an aria by building up to it:
beginning a scene with a slow or pensive one-part aria
(arioso), followed by a recitative that transforms the
dramatic situation and a full aria for the same character
discharging the accumulated emotion, he evolved the
cavatina–cabaletta design of Romantic opera. He
sometimes defeated an unconvincing happy end by setting the *coro* to tragic music, regardless of the words,
where the losing cause won his sympathy (for example
in *Amadigi*, *Tamerlano* and *Imeneo*). With increasing
frequency, especially after 1725, he linked the *coro* with
one or more preceding movements, whether arias,
dances or ensembles, by means of common thematic
material, an anticipation of the extended finales of subsequent practice. In some of the later operas (*Ariodante*,
Alcina, the third version of *Il pastor fido*) he used a
genuine chorus and a ballet; his integration of these
resources and the important element of spectacle into
the dramatic action should, in a sensitive production,
make an immediate appeal to a modern audience.

Once he had achieved maturity in *Agrippina* Handel's
operatic style changed little in 30 years, apart from the
assimilation of new influences already mentioned. At all

periods he wrote operas of different types. The commonest, as in all 18th-century *opera seria*, is heroic in temper with a plot taken from Roman or Greek history or occasionally from mythology or the Dark Ages. The characters are concerned with love, jealousy, dynastic rivalry and the grasp of power; though they often utter lofty sentiments, their politics are purely personal (no representative of the common people appears). This type of libretto became standardized in the work of Metastasio, a great poet whose artificial symmetry and literary refinement, though immensely popular with composers (and singers) who did not look beyond the confines of the aria, eventually blocked the progress of opera as an art and demanded the surgery of Gluck. Handel's three Metastasio operas (*Siroe*, *Poro* and *Ezio*) show him inspired by the poetry but inhibited by the stiffness of the characters. In his finest heroic operas plot, characters and musical invention are perfectly matched; the three masterpieces of 1724–5, *Giulio Cesare*, *Tamerlano* and *Rodelinda*, far surpass the work of any contemporary. The 'magic operas', though only five in number, are an important and distinctive class; two of them, *Orlando* and *Alcina*, are among the supreme examples of the form, and the other three (*Rinaldo*, *Teseo* and *Amadigi*) contain much superb music, especially in the scenes of sorcery and witchcraft. The supernatural element reduced the need for the plot to assume a rational course, admitted the poetic symbolism of the fairy tale, and released the romantic strain in Handel's imagination. The much prized machinery of the Baroque theatre came into its own in the spectacular transformation scenes.

A third type of opera embraces serious emotion, comic or even farcical situations and an element of parody, mocking the conventions of *opera seria* (including the castrato hero); these anti-heroic works, especially *Agrippina*, *Flavio*, *Partenope* and *Serse*, distil a characteristic and individual flavour. The ability to suggest the profound, the commonplace and the ridiculous aspects of human behaviour, not only in the same opera but in the same scene and situation, places Handel beside Monteverdi and Mozart as a master of dramatic irony on many levels. The spirit of playful comedy is not absent from Handel's most serious operas: Asteria twits her lover's apparent faithlessness in *Tamerlano*, Cleopatra turns her brutal and lascivious brother into a figure of fun, and Alexander the Great's duplicity is hilariously exposed when each of the two women he is courting, having overheard his advances to the other, quotes back at him in a different key the love music he addressed to her rival. This comprehensiveness of mood and dramatic approach gives his operas a depth seldom attained in the history of the art. But their quality can emerge only from productions based on a complete understanding of the convention.

15. Oratorios

Handel's final achievement, which contributed more than anything else to his lasting fame, was the creation of the English oratorio. It was a new form, only remotely connected with any of the continental varieties, and his single major innovation. He evolved it by accident, thanks to his reluctance to abandon the theatre, the Bishop of London's intervention against stage performance and the middle-class English public's appreciation of familiar Bible stories treated in an epic style that combined entertainment with edification. The evolution was gradual, though some of the advantages were obvious from the first: Handel was freed from the expense of scenery and costumes, and later from dependence on costly virtuoso singers, and he could make much greater use of the chorus to extend the musical and dramatic range and vary the texture. His chorus, all male, was small in numbers (probably not more than 20, including six boys for the treble part), but they were professionals from the Chapel Royal and Westminster Abbey, and the soloists were expected to sing with them.

Handel carried into the oratorio many structural devices from opera, especially articulation by tonality, but could afford to relax such conventions as the da capo aria since there were no exits. Nevertheless, especially in the first important oratorios, *Athalia* and *Saul*, the da capo remained valuable as a threat; by leading the ear to expect it, and either breaking off or continuing with something else, Handel could make dramatic points musically explicit. In *Athalia* (based, like *Esther*, on Racine) he linked airs and choruses in a remarkable profusion of new compound forms; in *Saul* he used five orchestral symphonies, all in the key of the overture and final chorus, to mark changes of scene and the passage of time and to unify the musical structure. Their strong mimetic quality (each depicts an important event in the story) suggests that Handel thought of them as a musical equivalent of the spectacular scene changes in the opera house; they lend themselves easily to modern stage production.

Most of the oratorios are dramas ('oratorio or sacred drama' was the regular description in the librettos), with the chorus, representing the Israelite nation and sometimes their opponents as well, playing a central part in the action and on occasion drawing a moral. This double posture is a product of their descent from Greek tragedy through Racine's *Esther* and *Athalie*, a link carefully preserved in most of the later oratorios. The moral is dramatic, arising from the conflict presented in the plot, not religious. All the major dramatic oratorios have a central theme derived from the facts of human experience: the undermining of judgment and sanity by envy or sexual jealousy, the clash of opposed cultures, the enfeeblement of the rulers' will as an empire decays, the choice between betrayal of principle and martyrdom, Man's enforced submission to a higher destiny and the limitations of mortality. These conflicts are enacted by individuals to whom Handel extended the profound sympathy for every human weakness that informs his operas. If the oratorios are grander in scale, it is because the chorus adds an extra dimension. Their national survival or rehabilitation depends on the fate of their leaders; they are personally involved in the struggles that engage Saul, Samson, Belshazzar,

13. Autograph MS from the air 'Take the heart you fondly gave', from Handel's oratorio 'Jephtha', composed 1751

Theodora and Jephtha. The greatest of the dramatic
oratorios thus possess a double plot held together by a
single theme. To the intricate skill with which this is
achieved Handel added an unusual power of characteriz-
ing nations as well as individuals. In *Athalia, Samson,
Alexander Balus* and *Theodora*, and in one scene
in *Deborah*, he depicted two peoples in sharply
differentiated music; in *Belshazzar*, the grandest of all
the oratorios, there are three. He did not load the dice;
he gave the heathen races some of the most ravishing
music, especially in *Athalia* and *Theodora*. This refusal
to make the righteous more sympathetic than the un-
righteous, evidence of his dramatic detachment and
freedom from sectarian bias, has been a constant
stumbling-block to those who sought to turn him into a
pillar of the moral establishment.

Not all the oratorios belong to this type. The choral
epic *Israel in Egypt* and *Messiah* stand apart. Neither
has a plot in the ordinary sense, and they are the only
oratorios whose words are taken exclusively from the
Bible. For this reason they became the most popular,
ousting works of at least comparable merit, and dis-
torted the image of the form. *Israel in Egypt* is justly
renowned for the grandeur of its choruses; but, apart
from the unevenness caused by the wholesale borrowings, it is not a well-balanced work owing to the slight
proportion of solo music. The greatness of *Messiah* –
Handel's only sacred oratorio in the true sense and
therefore untypical – derives on one level from its
unique fusion of the traditions of Italian opera, English
anthem and German Passion, and on another from the
coincidence of Handel's personal faith and creative
genius to express, more fully than in any other work of
art, the deepest aspirations of the Anglican religious

spirit. It remains nonetheless an 'entertainment' (Jennens's word), on however lofty a level, not an act of worship.

The classical dramas *Semele* and *Hercules*, though performed in the manner of oratorios, were not so called by Handel. Like *Acis and Galatea* they are closer to opera, with the chorus playing a smaller part than in the Old Testament works. In *Semele*, where the moral is implicit in the action and never openly stated, Handel's affinity with Homer breaks free in one of the most perfect artistic re-creations of the classical spirit; gods and heroes operate on the same level and are subject to the same weaknesses and temptations as the man in the street. *Hercules* re-creates the dramatic and moral force of Sophoclean tragedy in terms that underlie Handel's whole conception of the oratorio. In freshness of invention and imaginative scope the two have few rivals in Handel's work and none in English musical drama outside it. Some of the later oratorios, especially those with texts by Morell, are hampered by perfunctory plots, flabby diction and an excess of abstract moralizing. While this should not be regarded as automatically inhibiting Handel's response, a certain weakening becomes apparent, and a greater resort to borrowing. However, he recovered his powers in *Solomon*, whose hieratical double choruses are balanced by the casting of the principal soloists (including the hero) for women's voices and the vivid treatment of the personal drama in Act 2. In *Susanna* the balance is less successful; but the idyllic setting and the interplay of innocence and menace in the plot, comedy and tragedy in the characterization, and opera, oratorio and pastoral masque in the style give the work a peculiar fascination. The last two oratorios strike the profoundest note of all, inspired no doubt by the aging composer's consciousness of infirmity and approaching death. The mawkishness of the text of *Theodora* is entirely belied by the music, which draws a strong and subtle portrait of the Christian martyrs and makes the tragic end all the more moving by portraying the Romans (apart from Valens) as puzzled sensualists impressed despite themselves by the steadfast courage of their victims. In *Jephtha* the mighty chromatic choruses, full of agony and despair, seem to identify the composer with the central figure's enforced submission to an inexorable fate. The contrived *deus ex machina* solves nothing; what remains in the mind is Jephtha's heroic suffering and the wonderfully tender portrait of his daughter Iphis. If these two oratorios have a stronger Christian content than any earlier work except *Messiah*, Handel celebrates to the last the precarious joys and sorrows of humanity.

16. Posthumous reputation

Handel has been greatly misrepresented by posterity.
The seeds were sown while he was alive, when evan-
gelical piety claimed to discover a kindred spirit in the
oratorios. Hawkins and Burney revered him as a composer of immense dignity, the architect of the sublime;
they saw the humour of the man, but not of the music. It
was this portentous figure, the great choral composer,
that Haydn and Beethoven admired and occasionally
echoed, and who inspired Mozart's rescoring of
Messiah and other works. The Commemoration
Festival of 1784 in Westminster Abbey set the seal on
mammoth performances by outsize choirs and
orchestras that were to persist for a century and a half.
As if Handel had not left enough oratorios, steps were
taken to concoct others (*Gideon, Nabal, Redemption,
Omnipotence*) from his anthems and opera arias,
equipped with sacred words. From this it was no long
step to the conviction, voiced in 1862, that 'all Handel's
fine Italian airs [are] essentially of a sacred character'.
Although it was a Victorian, Edward Fitzgerald, who
with sure insight called him 'a good old Pagan at heart'
(a judgment that in no way impugns the sincerity of his
Christian beliefs), this prince of public entertainers, a
pantheist and hedonist who loved to depict the sensual
pleasures, not least when they transgressed the stricter
ethical principles, and who was repelled by the barren
negativity of the Puritan, was by a singular irony transformed into a marble monument of respectability, a
moral lawgiver clad in a massive wig with his finger

pointing at the heavens.

That conception is not entirely dead, perhaps because *Messiah* in some quarters retains the quality of a fetish. Many smaller men than Mozart have felt free to tinker with the scoring of this most professionally accomplished of composers. Prout, Harty, Beecham, Sargent and many others were convinced that they were strengthening Handel's message, whereas in fact they were falsifying it and in the long run antagonizing his potential public. Although the additional accompaniments have disappeared, Handel still has the reputation of emptying a theatre or concert hall. His dramatic works, performed with success by universities and private societies, seldom appear in national opera houses outside Germany; and when they do they are generally deformed by producers who try to adapt them either to what they think a modern audience will swallow with least discomfort or to some extraneous and usually impertinent interpretation of their own. In Germany (except at Göttingen since 1968) they are subjected to distortions of texture, especially in the pitch of the voice parts, and a denial of the recognized conventions of appoggiaturas and ornamentation that would scarcely be tolerated in Bach or Mozart. Scholarship has been slow to come to grips with Handel; when it has done so, and when its findings have seeped through the slow minds of impresarios into the public domain, a world of humane wisdom, profound art and aesthetic pleasure will become available to the widest audience.

The practice of staging the oratorios, also begun in Germany and greatly extended in Britain, notably at Cambridge between the wars, demands special mention. It can be justified by the essentially dramatic content of the works (with a few obvious exceptions) and by the congenital tendency of Handel's imagination to work in terms of the theatre. But a wary approach is required of the producer. Had Handel staged the oratorios after the manner of his operas, he would never have given such prominence to the chorus, if only because this would have laid an intolerable burden on the memory of his choristers. But the presence of substantial choruses, even elaborate fugal structures, does not of itself make the oratorios unstageworthy. The method used at Cambridge, with the main body of the chorus seated in the orchestra and smaller groups on stage (miming and dancing as well as singing), not only proved highly effective; it was based on two impeccable precedents, the Crown and Anchor performances of *Esther* in 1732 (which adopted the same method and might have been followed by Handel but for the Bishop of London's intervention) and the tradition of Greek tragedy underlying the whole form, in which a singing chorus played the double role of participants and commentators. While there is no question of staged oratorio replacing the traditional manner of performance, its conspicuous success undoubtedly drew attention to the principal source of Handel's inspiration.

17. Editions

While much of Handel's music became available in print during his life, the only works (other than purely instrumental music) issued complete were *Alexander's Feast* (1738), *Acis and Galatea* (1743) and a few anthems. After his death John Walsh and his successors published most of the English oratorios in full score, beginning with *Samson* (1763) and *Messiah* (1767). In 1786 Samuel Arnold issued proposals for publishing by subscription a collected edition, the first for any composer. It appeared between 1787 and 1797 in 180 numbered parts, but was by no means complete (only five Italian operas were included); despite many inaccuracies, it contains, especially in the appendices of the oratorio volumes, many items never since reprinted. The short-lived English Handel Society (1843), founded 'for the production of a superior and standard edition of the works of Handel', prepared 16 volumes of oratorios, anthems and duets (issued up to 1858); apart from G. A. Macfarren's *Belshazzar* they improve only slightly on Arnold's text.

The Händel-Gesellschaft (German Handel Society) edition, produced almost single-handed by Friedrich Chrysander, is so far the most complete. Between 1858 and 1902, 93 volumes were published, together with several revised versions (particularly vols.xxxii, lviii and part of xlviii), two autograph facsimiles – *Jephtha* (1885) and *Messiah* (1892) – and six supplementary works by other composers from which Handel made significant borrowings. Volume xlix (Miscellaneous

Vocal Music) was never issued, but some plates were engraved and offprints from them published by Moeck in 1960. Although Chrysander had access to the autographs, his principal source was the recently discovered collection of performing scores in the Hamburg Staats- und Universitätsbibliothek. Although a remarkable achievement for its date, his edition is weakened by his arbitrary selection of material in the more complex works and his failure to explain his methods. Certain of his decisions, such as the renumbering of the opp.1 and 2 sonatas to include works that did not originally belong to those collections, caused confusion which still persists.

A few smaller works, such as the Aylesford pieces for harpsichord and the nine German songs, were added individually to the canon. In 1955 the city of Halle, Handel's birthplace, saw the inauguration of a new project, the Hallische Händel-Ausgabe (Halle Handel Edition). At first intended merely to supplement Chrysander with reissues, vocal scores and other performing material, in 1958 it was transformed into a full critical edition. This change of policy, and in early years a failure to grasp the size of the task and the full extent of the sources, has resulted in a varying standard of reliability in the volumes so far issued.

WORKS

(for complete list of prints, see Smith, 1960)

Editions: G. F. Händels Werke: Ausgabe der Deutschen Händelgesellschaft, ed. F. W. Chrysander, i–xlviii, l–xcvi, suppls.i–vi (Leipzig and Bergedorf bei Hamburg, 1858–94, 1902/R1965) [HG]

Hallische Händel-Ausgabe im Auftrage der Georg Friedrich Händel-Gesellschaft, ed. M. Schneider, R. Steglich and others (Kassel, 1955–) [in progress] [HHA]

Not included in the list are numerous autograph sketches and fragments in *GB-Lbm* and *Cfm*, and unpublished doubtful or spurious works; MS sources cited include only major MS collections, important isolated MSS and available sources containing autograph material. [R] added to *GB-Lbm* distinguishes the Royal Music Library collection (see Squire, 1927) from that of the Department of Manuscripts (see Hughes-Hughes, 1906–9).

‡ – printed word-book extant
* – contains autograph material

† – contains performing score or other MSS with autograph annotations

Numbers in the right-hand column denote references in the text.

CG – Covent Garden, London
KT – King's/Queen's Theatre, Haymarket, London
LF – Lincoln's Inn Fields, London

NMH – New Music Hall, Fishamble Street, Dublin
SGG – Teatro S Giovanni Grisostomo, Venice
TG – Theater am Gänsemarkt, Hamburg

STAGE

Operas and related works

102

Title (Libretto)	MS sources	Performances under composer (no.)	Remarks	HG	HHA	
Almira [Der in Krohnen erlangte Glücks-Wechsel oder Almira, Königin von Castilien] (F. C. Feustking, after G. Pancieri)	D-B	TG, 8 Jan 1705 (?:20)‡	some music lost	lv	[ii/1]	3, 4, 21, 102
Nero [Die durch Blut und Mord erlangte Liebe] (Feustking)	—	TG, 25 Feb 1705 (?3)‡	music lost	—		4
Rodrigo [Vincer se stesso è la maggior vittoria] (F. Silvani: Il duello d'Amore e di Vendetta, adapted)	A-Wm, GB-Cfm, *Lbm[R], Mp	Florence, Cocomero Theatre, cNov 1707‡	some music lost	lvi	[ii/2]	6, 8
Der beglückte Florindo; Die verwandelte Daphne (H. Hinsch)	Mp (frag.)	TG, Jan 1708‡	written as one opera but perf. separately; music almost all lost, but see 'Other orchestral'	—		
Agrippina (V. Grimani)	A-Wn, GB-BENcoke, *Cfm, *Lbm[R], Lbm, Mp	SGG, cJan 1710 (?27)‡	1 aria pr. in Songs in . . . Etearco (London, 1711); ov. and 1 aria in Songs in . . . Antiochus (London, 1712); 1 aria in Songs	lvii	[ii/3]	9, 10, 11, 12, 17, 82, 104, 106

			in … Hamlet (London, 1712)			
Rinaldo (G. Rossi, based on scenario by A. Hill after Tasso: La Gerusalemme liberata)	†D-Hs, GB-BENcoke, *Cfm, *Lbm[R], Lbm, Lcm, Mp	KT. 24 Feb 1711 (15)‡ / KT. 23 Jan 1712 (9) / KT. 6 May 1713 (2) / KT. 30 Dec 1714 (11) / KT. 5 Jan 1717 (10)‡ / KT. 6 April 1731 (6)‡	rev., 4/5 new arias / rev., many addns from other operas	lviii (2 edns.)	[ii/4]	14, 15, 16, 17, 23, 37, 76, 105
Il pastor fido (Rossi, after B. Guarini)	†D-Hs, *GB-Cfm, †*Lbm[R], Lbm, Lcm, Mp, US-Wc	KT. 22 Nov 1712 (7)‡ / KT. 18 May 1734 (13)‡	? 1 aria added during run / rev., many addns incl. choruses from other works and 2 new arias	lix	[ii/5]	16, 17, 42, 93, 104
		KT. 9 Nov 1734 (5)‡	further rev., ballet, prol (Terpsicore) dances and 2 arias added		[ii/31]	
Teseo (N. F. Haym, after P. Quinault: Thésée)	GB-BENcoke, Cfm, *Lbm[R], Lbm, Mp, T	KT. 10 Jan 1713 (13)‡	last perf. incl. addns (?2 new arias)	lx	[ii/6]	16, 17, 93, 105
Silla (Rossi)	*Cfm, *Lbm[R], Lbm, Mp	? KT or Burlington House. 2 June 1713 (?1)‡	misattrib. G. Bononcini in GB-Lbm Add 5334	lxi	[ii/7]	16, 93
Amadigi di Gaula (Haym, after A. H. de la Motte: Amadis de Grèce)	†D-Hs, GB-BENcoke, *Cfm, *Lbm[R], Lbm, Lcm, Mp, T, US-Wc	KT. 25 May 1715 (6)‡	autograph lost (MS, said to be autograph, sold by Puttick & Simpson, London, 15 Dec 1879); arias added during run	lxii	ii/8	16, 17, 20, 23, 86, 94, 104, 105
		KT. 16 Feb 1716 (6)	5th perf. (20 June) incl. 2 new syms.			
		KT. 16 Feb 1717 (5)	3rd perf. incl. unidentified 'new scene'			
Radamisto (Haym, adapted from D. Lalli: L'amor tirannico, o Zenobia, as rev. for Florence, 1712)	D-Bds, †Hs, GB-BENcoke, *Cfm, *Lbm[R], Lbm, Lcm, Mp	KT. 27 April 1720 (10)‡ / KT. 28 Dec 1720 (7)‡ / KT. 25 Nov 1721 (4)	rev., 13 new items	lxiii	[ii/9]	37, 29, 31, 32, 76, 102
Muzio Scevola (P. A. Rolli, adapted from S. Stampiglia, as rev. for Vienna, 1710)	†D-Hs, GB-BENcoke, Cfm, *Lbm[R], Lbm, Mp, J-Tn	KT. Jan–Feb 1728 (c5)‡ / KT. 15 April 1721 (10)‡	further revs., 1 aria added only Act 3 by Handel; Act 1, F. Amadei; Act 2, G. Bononcini	lxiv	[ii/10]	30
		KT. 7 Nov 1722 (3)	rev. and shortened			

Title (Libretto)	MS sources	Performances under composer (no.)	Remarks	HG	HHA	
Floridante (Rolli, adapted from Silvani: La Costanza in trionfo, ? as rev. for Livorno, 1706)	†D-Hs, GB-Cfm, *Lbm[R], Mp	KT, 9 Dec 1721 (15)‡ KT, 4 Dec 1722 (7) KT, 29 April 1727 (2) KT, 3 March 1733 (7)‡	5 arias added, 2 new shortened, 2 new arias (MS word-book amendments Lbm) 1727 version rev. and shortened	lxv	lii/11]	29, 30, 40
Ottone, Rè di Germania (Haym, adapted from S. B Pallavicino: Teofane)	†D-Hs, GB-BENcoke, *Cfm, DRc. *Lbm[R], Lbm, †Ob	KT, 12 Jan 1723 (14)‡ KT, 11 Dec 1723 (6) KT, 8 Feb 1726 (8)‡ KT, 11 April 1727 (2) KT, 13 Nov 1733 (4)‡	last 3 perfs. with 4 new arias rev., 5 new arias rev., 3 arias and new duet added	lxvi	[ii/12]	27, 29, 31, 32, 33, 41, 43, 82, 86, 93, 94
Flavio, Rè di Longobardi (Haym, adapted from M. Noris: Flavio Cuniberto, as rev. for Rome, 1696)	†D-Hs, GB-BENcoke, Cfm, *Lbm[R], Lbm, *Mp	KT, 14 May 1723 (8)‡ KT, 18 April 1732 (4)‡	much rev.	lxvii	[ii/13]	29, 31, 32, 106
Giulio Cesare in Egitto (Haym, adapted from G. F. Bussani)	†D-Hs, GB-BENcoke, †*Cfm, *Lbm[R], Lbm, Mp	KT, 20 Feb 1724 (13)‡ KT, 2 Jan 1725 (10)‡ KT, 17 Jan 1730 (11)‡	rev., 4 new arias; 2 more added during run further revs., 2 new arias added during run (MS word-book amendments Lbm)	lxviii	[ii/14]	22, 31, 32, 37, 83, 86, 105
Tamerlano (Haym, adapted from A. Piovene and rev. version: Il Bajazete, 1719, after N. Pradon: Tamerlan)	†D-Hs, *GB-Lbm[R], Lbm, Mp	KT, 1 Feb 1732 (4) KT, 31 Oct 1724 (12)‡ KT, 13 Nov 1731 (3)‡	shortened, but 1 new aria	lxix	[ii/15]	22, 32, 103, 104, 105, 106
Rodelinda, Regina de' Longobardi (Haym, adapted from A. Salvi, after P. Corneille: Pertharite)	†D-Hs, *GB-Cfm, *Lbm[R], Lbm, Mp	KT, 13 Feb 1725 (14)‡ KT, 18 Dec 1725 (8) KT, 4 May 1731 (8)	4 new arias and new duet (MS word-book amendments Lbm) 2 arias and duet added from other operas	lxx	[ii/16]	22, 32, 37, 105

Work	Sources	Performances	Notes		
Scipione (Rolli, adapted from Salvi)	†D-Hs, †GB-Cfm, *Lbm[R], Lbm, Mp	KT, 12 March 1726 (13)‡ KT, 3 Nov 1730 (6)‡	rev. with 14 added items incl. 2 new arias	lxxi	[ii/17] 33
Alessandro (Rolli, adapted from O. Mauro: La superbia d'Alessandro)	†D-Hs, GB-BENcoke, Cfm, *Lbm[R], Lbm, Mp	KT, 5 May 1726 (13)‡ KT, 26 Dec 1727 (over 3) KT, 25 Nov 1732 (6)‡	new aria added during run shortened revived as Rossane, KT. 1743‡, 1744, 1748‡, probably with Handel's cooperation	lxxii	[ii/18] 33, 57 57, 63
Admeto, Rè di Tessaglia (adapted from A. Aureli: L'Antigona delusa da Alceste, as rev. Mauro for Hanover, 1681)	BENcoke, Cfm, *Lbm[R], Lbm, Mp	KT, 31 Jan 1727 (19)‡ KT, 30 Sept 1727 (6) KT, 25 May 1728 (3)‡ KT, 7 Dec 1731 (6)‡	autograph and perf. scores lost; new aria added during run	lxxiii	[ii/19] 33, 34, 69, 103
Riccardo Primo, Rè d'Inghilterra (Rolli, adapted from F. Briani: Isacio tiranno)	D-Hs, *GB-Cfm, *Lbm[R], Lbm, Mp, Ob	KT, 11 Nov 1727 (11)‡	new aria rev., 6 arias added, 3 new	lxxiv	[ii/20] 34
[Genserico/Olibrio] (after N. Beregan: Il Genserico, as rev. for Hamburg, 1693)	*Cfm, *Lbm[R]		only pt. of Act 1 drafted; music mostly used in Siroe and Tolomeo	—	—
Siroe, Rè di Persia (Haym, adapted from Metastasio, as rev. for Naples, 1727)	B-Bc, †D-Hs, GB-Cfm, *Lbm[R], Lbm, Mp	KT, 17 Feb 1728 (18)‡		lxxv	[ii/21] 34, 105
Tolomeo, Rè di Egitto (Haym, adapted from C. S. Capece: Tolomeo e Alessandro)	†D-Hs, GB-Cfm, *Lbm[R], Lcm, Mp	KT, 30 April 1728 (7)‡ KT, 19 May 1730 (7)‡ KT, 2 Jan 1733 (4)‡	much rev. with 12 added items 6 further addns	lxxvi	[ii/22] 34
Lotario (adapted from Salvi: Adelaide, as rev. for Venice, 1729)	†D-Hs, *GB-Cfm, *Lbm[R], Lbm, Mp	KT, 2 Dec 1729 (10)‡		lxxvii	[ii/23] 37
Partenope (adapted from Stampiglia, as rev. for Venice, 1707)	†D-Hs, GB-BENcoke, *Cfm, *Lbm[R], Mp	KT, 24 Feb 1730 (7)‡ KT, 12 Dec 1730 (7) CG, 29 Jan 1737 (4)‡	rev., new aria shortened and rearranged	lxxviii	37, 106 [ii/24]
Poro, Rè dell'Indie (adapted from Metastasio: Alessandro nell'Indie)	†D-Hs, GB-BENcoke, *Cfm, *Lbm[R], Mp	KT, 2 Feb 1731 (16)‡ KT, 23 Nov 1731 (4)‡ KT, 8 Dec 1736 (4)‡	rev., 3 arias added rev., 6 arias added (1 by L. Vinci, 2 by G. A. Ristori)	lxxix	[ii/25] 37, 105

Title (Libretto)	MS sources	Performances under composer (no.)	Remarks	HG	HHA
[Tito] (from unknown source, after Racine: Bérénice)	*Lbm[R]		only Act 1 scenes i–iii composed, entitled Titus l'Empereur, music partly used in Ezio	—	
Ezio (adapted from Metastasio)	†D-Hs, GB-Cfm, *Lbm[R], Mp	KT, 15 Jan 1732 (5)‡		lxxx	[ii/26] 37, 105
Sosarme, Rè di Media (adapted from Salvi: Dionisio, Rè di Portogallo)	†D-Hs, GB-BENcoke, Cfm, *Lbm[R], Mp	KT, 15 Feb 1732 (11)‡ KT, 27 April 1734 (3)	shortened, but 4 arias added	lxxxi	[ii/27] 37, 42
Orlando (adapted from Capece, after L. Ariosto: Orlando furioso)	D-Hs, GB-Cfm, *Lbm[R], Lbm, Mp	KT, 27 Jan 1733 (10)‡		lxxxii	ii/28 4, 40, 103, 105
Arianna in Creta (adapted from P. Pariati: Arianna e Teseo, as rev. for Naples, 1721, and Rome, 1729)	†D-Hs, GB-BENcoke, *Cfm, *Lbm[R], Mp	KT, 26 Jan 1734 (17)‡ CG, 27 Nov 1734 (5)‡	rev., 2 arias, 1 new, and ballet music added	lxxxiii	[ii/29] 41, 42
Oreste (adapted from G. Barlocci)	D-Hs, GB-Mp	CG, 18 Dec 1734 (3)‡	pasticcio, music by Handel incl. new recits and ballet music	xlviii, 102 (ov.)	42
Ariodante (adapted from Salvi: Ginevra, Principessa di Scozia, after Ariosto: Orlando furioso)	†D-Hs, *GB-Cfm, *Lbm[R], Lbm, Mp	CG, 8 Jan 1735 (11)‡ CG, 5 May 1736 (2)	incl. ballet music	lxxxv	[ii/32] 4, 42, 45, 104
Alcina (adapted from L'isola di Alcina, 1728, after Ariosto: Orlando furioso)	†D-Hs, *GB-Cfm, *Lbm[R], Lbm, Mp	CG, 16 April 1735 (18)‡ CG, 6 Nov 1736 (3)‡ CG, 10 June 1737 (2)	dances omitted; 7 arias added (none by Handel)	lxxxvi	[ii/33] 43, 45, 104, 105
Atalanta (adapted from B. Valeriano: La caccia in Etolia)	D-Hs, GB-BENcoke, Cfm, *Lbm[R], Mp	CG, 12 May 1736 (8)‡ CG, 20 Nov 1736 (2)	incl. ballet music dances omitted	lxxxvii	[ii/34] 45
Arminio (adapted from Salvi)	†D-Hs, GB-BENcoke, *Cfm, *Lbm[R], Mp	CG, 12 Jan 1737 (6)‡		lxxxviii	[ii/35] 46
Giustino (adapted from Beregan, as rev. Pariati for Rome, 1724)	D-Hs, *GB-Cfm, *Lbm[R], Lbm, Mp	CG, 16 Feb 1737 (9)‡		lxxxix	[ii/36] 46
Berenice (adapted from Salvi)	†D-Hs, *GB-Cfm, *Lbm[R], Mp	CG, 18 May 1737 (4)‡		xc	[ii/37] 46
Faramondo (adapted from A. Zeno, as rev. for Rome, 1720)	†D-Hs, *GB-Cfm, *Lbm[R], Mp	KT, 3 Jan 1738 (8)‡		xci	[ii/38] 47, 48
Alessandro Severo (adapted from Zeno, as rev. for Milan, 1723)	D-Hs, *GB-Cfm, Lbm[R], Lbm	KT, 25 Feb 1738 (6)‡	pasticcio, music by Handel, incl. new ov. and recits	xlviii, 104 (ov.)	48

Title (Libretto)	MS sources	Performances (no.)	Remarks			
Serse (adapted from N. Minato, as rev. Stampiglia for Rome, 1694)	D-Hs, *GB-Cfm, *Lbm[R], Mp	KT, 15 April 1738 (5)‡	pasticcio semi-staged; new recits, 5 arias and final chorus	xcii	ii/39	5, 48, 81, 82, 106
Giove in Argo (adapted from A. M. Lucchini)	*Cfm, *Lbm[R], Mp	KT, 1 May 1739 (2)‡	drafted Sept 1738, rev. for perf. Oct 1740	—	[ii/40]	49, 52, 53, 103, 104
Imeneo (adapted from Stampiglia)	†D-Hs, *GB-Cfm, *Lbm[R], Lbm, Mp	LF, 22 Nov 1740 (2)‡; NMH, 24 March 1742 (2)‡	concert perf. as serenata; many cuts, but 2 arias and 2 duets added	xciii		
Deidamia (Rolli)	†D-Hs, *GB-Cfm, *Lbm[R], Lbm, Mp	LF, 10 Jan 1741 (3)‡		xciv	[ii/41]	32, 52

Arrangements of operas by other composers
(not in HG or HHA: KT – King's Theatre, Haymarket, London)

Title (Libretto)	MS sources	Performances (no.)	Remarks
Elpidia (A. Zeno: Li rivali generosi, adapted)	†GB-Lbm	KT, 11 May 1725 (12)‡, 30 Nov 1725 (4)	pasticcio mainly from L. Vinci: Ifigenia in Tauride and La Rosmira fedele, and G. F. Orlandini: Berenice, Venice, 1725; perf. Nov 1725 with revs.
Ormisda (Zeno, adapted)	D-Hs, GB-BENcoke, †Lbm	KT, 4 April 1730 (13)‡. 24 Nov 1730 (5)	pasticcio with arias by Vinci, J. A. Hasse, Orlandini and others; revs. incl. in word-book, GB-Lbm
Venceslao (Zeno, adapted)	†D-Hs	KT, 12 Jan 1731 (4)‡	pasticcio with arias by Vinci, Hasse, N. Porpora and others
Lucio Papirio (Zeno, rev. C. I. Frugoni)	†Hs, GB-Lam	KT, 23 May 1732 (4)‡	by G. Giacomelli, Parma, 1729, slightly adapted
Catone (Metastasio)	†D-Hs, †GB-Lam	KT, 4 Nov 1732 (5)‡	mostly by L. Leo, Venice, 1729, with arias by other composers
Semiramide (Metastasio)	†D-Hs, †GB-Cfm	KT, 30 Oct 1733 (4)‡	mostly by Vinci, with arias by other composers
Caio Fabbricio (Zeno)	†D-Hs	KT, 4 Dec 1733 (4)‡	mostly by Hasse, Rome, 1732, with arias by other composers
Arbace (Metastasio: Artaserse)	†Hs	KT, 8 Jan 1734 (8)‡	mostly by Vinci, with arias by other composers
Didone (Metastasio)	†GB-Lbm, †US-Cn	KT, 13 April 1737 (3)‡	mostly by Vinci, Rome, 1726

124

Theatre music

Title (Description)	MS sources	Performances (no.)	Remarks	HG	HHA	
The Alchemist (for Ben Jonson's play)	GB-Lbm, Mp	?King's Theatre, Haymarket, London, 14 Jan 1710 (2); later revivals	9 items, nos. 1, 3–9 from ov. to Rodrigo, no. 2 ('Prelude') probably not by Handel; pubd Walsh (London, 1710) attrib. 'an Italian master' (copy GB-BENcoke); see Price (1975)	—		61, 62
[Comus] (3 songs and trio to conclude private arr. of Milton: A Maske presented at Ludlow Castle, rev. J. Dalton)	Mp	Exton, Leics, June 1745 (1), 29 July 1748 (1)	music re-used in Occasional Oratorio; see Hicks (1976); ed. C. Timms and A. Hicks as Music for Comus (London, 1977)	—		
Alceste (masque or semi-opera, T. Smollett, after Euripides)	†D-Hs, *GB-Lbm[R], *Lbm, Lcm		composed Dec 1749–Jan 1750; music used in The Choice of Hercules; lib lost	xlviB	[i/30]	65, 66

CG – Covent Garden, London
FH – Foundling Hospital, London
KT – King's Theatre, Haymarket, London

LF – Lincoln's Inn Fields, London
NMH – New Music Hall, Fishamble Street, Dublin
OCC – Christ Church Hall, Oxford
OST – Sheldonian Theatre, Oxford

ODES, ORATORIOS, ETC

Title (Libretto)	MS sources	Performances under composer (no.)	Remarks	HG	HHA	
Il trionfo del Tempo e del Disinganno (B. Pamphili)	D-MÜs, *GB-Lbm[R]	? Rome, spr. 1707	D-MÜs's score copied by 14 May 1707	xxiv	[i/4]	7
Oratorio per la Resurrezione di Nostro Signor Gesù Cristo (C. S. Capece)	†D-MÜs, *GB-Cfm, Lbm, *Lbm[R], Mp, US-Cu, Wc	Rome, Palazzo Ruspoli, 8 April 1708 (2)‡		xxxix	[i/3]	7, 8, 11, 12
Ode for the Birthday of Queen Anne (Eternal source of light divine) (? A. Philips)	D-Hs, GB-Cfm, Lbm, *Lbm[R], US-Cu, NBu, PRu, Wc		probably Jan 1713 for perf. on 6 Feb but not perf.; rev. for 1714 celebration but again not perf.	xlviA	i/6	18
Der für die Sünde der Welt gemartete und sterbende Jesus [Brockes Passion] (B. H. Brockes)	A-Wgm, Wn, D-Bds, Hs, *GB-Lbm[R], Mp	? Hamburg, 1716‡	see Becker (1956) for Hamburg perfs., 1719–21	xv	i/7	81, 99

Title	Sources	Performances	Remarks			Pages
Acis and Galatea (J. Gay and others, after Ovid: Metamorphoses, xiii)	Cannons version: D-Hs, GB-BENcoke, DRc, Lbm, *Lbm[R], Mp, T, US-Wc; later versions: *GB-Cfm, †*Lbm, ††*Lbm[R], DRc, US-Wc	Cannons, Edgware, 1718, KT, 10 June 1732 (4)‡, 5 Dec 1732 (4); OCC, 11 July 1733 (1)‡; KT, 7 May 1734 (1); CG, 24 March 1736 (2); LF, 13 Dec 1739 (2)‡, 28 Feb 1741 (2); NMH, 20 Jan 1742 (2)	composed May 1718 (see Rogers, 1973), rev. for perfs. 1732-6 with added It. airs from cantata Sorge il dì (Aci, Galatea e Polifemo) and elsewhere	iii, liii	[i/9]	21, 24, 35, 39, 41, 42, 45, 51, 52, 53, 82, 83, 111, 116
Esther (? A. Pope and J. Arbuthnot, after Racine, trans. T. Brereton; with addns by S. Humphreys, 1732)	first version: D-Hs, *GB-Cfm, *Lbm[R], US-BETm, Wc, later versions: †D-Hs, GB-BENcoke, *Cfm, Lbm, *Lbm[R], Lcm, Mp, US-NYp	? Cannons, 1718; KT, 2 May 1732 (6)‡, 14 April 1733 (2)‡; OST, 5 July 1733 (2)‡; CG, 5 March 1735 (6), 7 April 1735 (2), 6 April 1737 (2); LF, 26 March 1740 (1); NMH, 3 Feb 1742 (3)‡; CG, 15 March 1751 (1)‡, 25 Feb 1757 (1)‡	extensively rev. for 1732 perf. with much new music; addns for 1735 perf. incl. org conc.	xl, xii	[i/8, i/10]	21, 24, 25, 35, 38, 43, 46, 51, 53, 70, 108, 115
Deborah (Humphreys, after Judges v)	†D-Hs, GB-Cfm, DRc, Lbm, *Lbm[R], Mp	KT, 17 March 1733 (6)‡; OST, 12 July 1733 (1); KT, 2 April 1734 (3); CG, 26 March 1735 (3); KT, 3 Nov 1744 (2)‡; CG, 8 March 1754 (2)‡, 19 March 1756 (1)‡	music partly from earlier works	xxix	[i/11]	21, 40, 42, 43, 46, 52, 60, 110
Athalia (Humphreys, after Racine)	†D-Hs, GB-BENcoke, *Cfm, Lbm, *Lbm[R], Lcm, Mp, J-Tn	OST, 10 July 1733 (2)‡; CG, 1 April 1735 (5), 5 March 1756 (3)‡	1735 perf. with much new music; 1756 perf. rev. with addns	v	[i/12]	21, 41, 42, 43, 62, 85, 86, 107, 110
Il Parnasso in festa (anon.)	†D-Hs, *GB-Cfm, Lbm, *Lbm[R]	KT, 13 March 1734 (5)‡; CG, 9 March 1737 (2); LF, 8 Nov 1740 (1)‡; KT, 14 March 1741 (1)	music mostly from Athalia; 1741 perf. ? not under Handel	liv	[ii/30]	42, 46, 52
Alexander's Feast (J. Dryden: Ode for St Cecilia's Day, 1697; addns from N. Hamilton: The Power of Music)	†D-Hs, GB-BENcoke, Cfm, DRc, Lbm, *Lbm[R], †Lcm, Mp	CG, 19 Feb 1736 (5)‡, 16 March 1737 (6); KT, 17 Feb 1739 (3)‡; LF, 22 Nov 1739 (2)‡; NMH, 17 Feb 1742 (2)‡; CG, 1 March 1751 (4)‡, 9 March 1753 (2)‡, 14 Feb 1755 (2)	1742 perf. with new solo (only bc extant) and duet; duet rev. 1751	xii	i/1	32, 46, 49, 50, 53, 68, 93, 96, 116

Title (Libretto)	MS sources	Performances under composer (no.)	Remarks	HG	HHA	
Il trionfo del Tempo e della Verità (Pamphili, with anon. addns)	†D-Hs, *GB-Cfm, Lbm, **Lbm[R], Mp	CG, 23 March 1737 (4)‡; KT, 3 March 1739 (1)	extensive rev. of Il trionfo del Tempo e del Disinganno with much new music	xx, xxiv	[i/4]	46, 50, 76
Saul (C. Jennens, after I Samuel xvii–II Samuel i and A. Cowley: Davideis)	†D-Hs, GB-Cfm, Lbm, *Lbm[R], Lcm, Mp, Ob	KT, 16 Jan 1739 (6)‡; LF, 21 March 1740 (1), 18 March 1741 (1)‡; NMH, 25 May 1742 (1)‡; CG, 16 March 1744 (2)‡; KT, 13 March 1745 (1); CG, 2 March 1750 (2)‡, 15 March 1754 (2)		xiii	i/13	43, 49, 51, 52, 54, 58, 60, 83, 85, 86, 107, 108
Israel in Egypt (mainly from Exodus xv and Prayer Book Psalter)	†D-Hs, GB-BENcoke, Cfm, DRc, Lbm, *Lbm[R], Mp	KT, 4 April 1739 (3)‡; LF, 1 April 1740 (1)‡; CG, 17 March 1756 (2)‡, 4 March 1757 (1)‡, 24 Feb 1758 (1)	perf. 1739 and 1740 with arr. of Funeral Anthem as pt.i; perf. 1756–8 with new pt.i, mostly from Solomon and Occasional Oratorio	xvi	[i/14]	49, 50, 51, 62, 69, 80, 85, 88, 110
Ode for St Cecilia's Day (From harmony, from heav'nly harmony) (Dryden)	†D-Hs, GB-BENcoke, Cfm, DRc, *Lbm[R], Lcm, Mp, US-PRu	LF, 22 Nov 1739 (2)‡, 13 Dec 1739 (2)‡, 21 Feb 1740 (2). 11 March 1741 (1), 8 April 1741 (1); NMH, 20 Jan 1742 (2)‡; CG, 18 March 1743 (1), 23 May 1754 (1), 21 Feb 1755 (1)		xxiii	[i/15]	50, 53
L'Allegro, il Penseroso ed il Moderato (Jennens, pts.i–ii compiled from Milton)	†D-Hs, GB-BENcoke, *Cfm, *Lbm[R], Mp	LF, 27 Feb 1740 (6)‡, 31 Jan 1741 (3)‡, 8 April 1741 (1); NMH, 23 Dec 1741 (1)‡, 13 Jan 1742 (2)‡; CG, 18 March 1743 (1), 23 May 1754 (1)‡, 21 Feb 1755 (1)	MS word-book US-SM; perf. Jan 1741 with 7 new items	vi	i/16	51, 52, 53, 61, 85

Work	Sources	Performances	Notes			
Messiah (compiled Jennens from the Bible and Prayer Book Psalter)	D-Hs, EIRE-Dm, Dtc, GB-BENcoke, *Cfm, Ckc, Lam, Lbm, *Lbm[R], Lu, Thomas Coram Foundation. London, Mp, †*T, US-NYpm	NMH, 13 April 1742 (2)‡; CG, 23 March 1743 (3)‡; KT, 9 April 1745 (2); CG, 23 March 1749 (1)‡; CG, FH, 13 April 1750 (3)‡; FH, 18 April 1751 (2); CG, FH, 25 March 1752 (3). 13 April 1753 (2). 5 April 1754 (2), 19 March 1755 (3)‡; 7 April 1756 (3). 30 March 1757 (3)‡, 10 March 1758 (4)‡; CG, 30 March 1759 (3)‡	2 solos added 1743 (But lo! and Their sound); Rejoice and Their sound reset ?1745; But who may abide and Thou art gone up reset 1750	xlv	i/17	52, 53, 54, 56, 57, 58, 66, 69, 70, 76, 79, 96, 101, 110, 112,113, 114, 116
Samson (adapted Hamilton from Milton: Samson Agonistes and other poems)	†D-Hs, GB-BENcoke, *Cfm, Ckc, Lbm, *Lbm[R], Mp, J-Tn	CG, 18 Feb 1743 (8)‡; 24 Feb 1744 (2)‡; KT, 1 March 1745 (2); CG, 3 March 1749 (4)‡, 4 April 1750 (2)‡, 6 March 1752 (3)‡, 4 April 1753 (3)‡, 29 March 1754 (1)‡, 26 Feb 1755 (2), 14 March 1759 (3)‡	mostly completed Sept-Oct 1741: MS word-book. †US-SM: 1 air added 1745; air from Occasional Oratorio added 1754	x	[i/18]	27, 53, 54, 55, 57, 58, 60, 86, 108, 116
Semele (W. Congreve, rev. with addns from his poems and from Pope: Summer, or Alexis)	†D-Hs, *GB-Cfm, *Lbm[R], Mp, US-Wc	CG, 10 Feb 1744 (4)‡; KT, 1 Dec 1744 (2)‡	MS word-book †US-SM. 6 airs added for Dec 1744, some in It.	vii	[i/19]	57, 58, 60, 82, 83, 86, 111
Joseph and his Brethren (J. Miller, after Genesis xlii-xliv)	†D-Hs, GB-BENcoke, *Cfm, Ckc, Lbm, *Lbm[R], Mp	CG, 2 March 1744 (4)‡; KT, 15 March 1745 (2)‡; CG, 20 March 1747 (2)‡, 28 Feb 1755 (1)‡, 9 March 1757 (1)‡		xlii	[i/20]	57, 58, 60
Hercules (T. Broughton, after Sophocles: Trachiniae and Ovid: Metamorphoses, ix)	†D-Hs, GB-BENcoke, Cfm, *Lbm[R], Mp	KT, 5 Jan 1745 (2)‡; CG, 24 Feb 1749 (2)‡, 21 Feb 1752 (2)‡		iv	[i/22]	58, 60, 86, 111
Belshazzar (Jennens, after Daniel v, Jeremiah, Isaiah, Herodotus: History, i, and Xenophon: Cyropaedia)	†D-Hs, GB-BENcoke, *Cfm, *Lbm[R], Mp, T, US-PRu	KT, 27 March 1745 (3)‡; CG, 22 Feb 1751 (2)‡, 22 Feb 1758 (1)‡	MS word-book, US-SM: some items rev. 1751: new air added 1758	xix	[i/21]	58, 59, 60, 70, 92, 101, 108, 110
Occasional Oratorio (Hamilton, compiled mainly from Milton's paraphrases of the Psalms, with lines from E. Spenser: The Faery Queen, Hymn of Heavenly Beauty, Tears of the Muses)	†D-Hs, GB-BENcoke, *Cfm, *Lbm[R]	CG, 14 Feb 1746 (3)‡, 6 March 1747 (3)	some of Acts 2-3 from other works, esp. Israel in Egypt; MS word-book (frag.), †US-SM: 1 air added 1747	xliii	[i/23]	58, 60, 86, 101

Title (Libretto)	MS sources	Performances under composer (no.)	Remarks	HG	HHA	
Judas Maccabaeus (T. Morell, after I Maccabees and Josephus: Antiquities, xii)	†D-Hs, *GB-Cfm, *Lbm[R], Mp	CG, 1 April 1747 (6)‡, 26 Feb 1748 (6)‡, 9 March 1750 (4)‡, 20 March 1751 (1)‡, 18 March 1752 (2)‡, 23 March 1753 (3)‡, 27 March 1754 (2), 12 March 1755 (2), 26 March 1756 (2)‡, 25 March 1757 (1)‡, 3 March 1758 (2)‡, 23 March 1759 (2)‡	MS word-book, †US-SM; items added during first run; further airs added in later perfs, incl. 2 new airs in 1758	xx	[i/24]	52, 62, 76, 79, 96
Joshua (?Morell)	†D-Hs, GB-BENcoke, *Cfm, DRc, *Lbm[R], Mp, US-PRu	CG, 9 March 1748 (4)‡, 14 Feb 1752 (2)‡, 22 March 1754 (1)‡	MS word-book, US-SM; 5 items added 1754	xvii	[i/26]	52, 63, 85, 96
Alexander Balus (Morell, after I Maccabees)	†D-Hs, *GB-Cfm, *Lbm[R], Mp, US-PRu	CG, 23 March 1748 (3)‡, 1 March 1754 (1)‡	MS word-book, †US-SM; rev. 1754, with added items from Alceste	xxxiii	[i/25]	63, 79, 83, 96, 110
Susanna (anon. after Apocrypha)	†D-Hs, *GB-Cfm, *Lbm[R], Mp	CG, 10 Feb 1749 (4)‡, 9 March 1759 (1)‡	MS word-book, †US-SM; shortened 1759, with added item from Semele	i	[i/28]	63, 70, 84, 111
Solomon (anon.. after II Chronicles, I Kings v and Josephus: Antiquities, viii)	D-Hs, *GB-Cfm, *Lbm[R], Mp	CG, 17 March 1749 (3)‡, 2 March 1759 (2)‡	MS word-book, US-SM; rearr. 1759, with 5 added airs	xxvi	[i/27]	63, 70, 85, 92, 111
Theodora (Morell, after R. Boyle: The Martyrdom of Theodora and Didymus)	†D-Hs, GB-Cfm, *Lbm[R], Mp	CG, 16 March 1750 (3)‡, 5 March 1755 (1)	MS word-book, †GB-Mp	viii	[i/29]	65, 75, 76, 82, 85, 110, 112
The Choice of Hercules (R. Lowth: The Judgement of Hercules, Glasgow, 1743, adapted)	†D-Hs, GB-Cfm, *Lbm, *Lbm[R], Mp	CG, 1 March 1751 (4)‡, 9 March 1753 (2)‡, 14 Feb 1755	music mostly from Alceste; MS word-book (frag.), US-SM	xxviii	i/31	66, 68
Jephtha (Morell, after Judges xi and G. Buchanan: Jephthes sive Votum, 1554)	†D-Hs, *GB-Cfm, Lbm, *Lbm[R], Mp	CG, 26 Feb 1752 (3)‡, 16 March 1753 (2)‡, 2 April 1756 (1), 1 March 1758 (1)‡	MS word-book, US-SM; air from Agrippina and qnt added 1753	xliv	[i/32]	66, 67, 69, 78, 87, 92, 109, 110, 112, 116
The Triumph of Time and Truth (Morell, after Pamphili: Il trionfo del Tempo, trans. G. Oldmixon)	D-Hs, GB-Lbm[R], T	CG, 11 March 1757 (4)‡, 10 Feb 1758 (2)‡	music mainly from Il trionfo del Tempo e della Verità, with addns from other works; 5 airs added 1758	xx	[i/33]	70

SACRED VOCAL

Latin church music

Title/first words, Key	Scoring	MS sources	Remarks	HG	HHA
Coelestis dum spirat aura, D/G, motet	S, 2 vn, bc	D-MÜs	for St Antony of Padua; perf. Vignanello, 13 June 1707; ed. R. Ewerhart (Cologne, 1957)	—	
Dixit Dominus (Ps cix), g	2 S, A, T, B, SSATB, 2 vn, 2 va, bc	MÜs, *GB-Lbm[R], Lcm, Mp, Ob	completed April 1707	xxxviii, 53	iii/1
Haec est regina virginum, ant	S, str, bc	formerly W. H. Cummings's private collection	lost; ?perf. Rome, S Maria di Monte Santo, 16 July 1707; see W. H. Cummings, MA, iii (1912), 116, and Hall, MT, c (1959)	—	
Laudate pueri Dominum (Ps cxii), F	S, 2 vn, bc	D-B, *GB-Lbm[R]	? Hamburg, c1706	xxxviii, 1	
Laudate pueri Dominum (Ps cxii), D	S, SSATB, 2 ob, 2 vn, 2 va, bc	*Lbm[R], Mp, Ob	completed Rome, 8 July 1707	xxxviii, 19	8
Nisi Dominus (Ps cxxvi), G	A, T, B, SSAATTBB, 4 vn, 2 va, bc	psalm only: Lbm[R], Lbm, Mp; doxology: D-MÜs	completed Rome, 13 June 1707; vocal score of doxology in Crystal Palace ... Handel Festival 1891: The Selection (London, 1891), and of complete work ed. T. W. Bourne (London, 1898); full score ed. S. Tsuji (Tokyo, 1928); for lost MSS see W. H. Cummings, MA, iii (1912), 116; MT, xlv (1904), 521 and liii (1912), 306	xxxviii, 127 (psalm only)	8
O qualis de caelo sonus, G, motet	S, 2 vn, bc	*MÜs	for Pentecost; perf. Vignanello, 12 June 1707; ed. R. Ewerhart (Cologne, 1957)	—	
Saeviat tellus inter rigores, D, motet	S, 2 ob, str, bc	GB-Lbm	for Our Lady of Mount Carmel; ? perf. Rome, S Maria di Monte Santo, 16 July 1707	—	
Salve regina, g, ant	S, 2 vn, vc, org, bc	*D-B	perf. Vignanello, 12 or 13 June 1707	xxxviii, 136	
Silete venti, Bb, motet	S, 2 ob, 2 bn, str, bc	*GB-Lbm[R]	? written for Venetian visit, 1729	xxxviii, 144	
Te decus virginem, ant	A, str, bc	formerly W. H. Cummings's private collection	as for Haec est regina	—	

Title/first words, Key	Scoring	MS sources	Remarks	HG	HHA
Alleluias, Amens:	S, bc		probably intended as vocal studies		
Alleluia . . . amen, d, d, G, a; Amen. F: Amen . . . alleluia. g		*GB-Lbm[R]		xxxviii, 166	
Alleluia . . . amen, F (2)		*Cfm	ed. A. Mann as *Two Sacred Arias* (New York, 1979)		25, 81, 93, 99

English church music
(parenthesized nos. after titles refer to HG)

Title/first words, Key	Scoring	MS sources	Remarks	HG	HHA
'Chandos' anthems:			composed 1717–18 at Cannons, Edgware, for James Brydges, created Duke of Chandos April 1719		
As pants the hart (6A), e	S, T, STB, ob, bn, 2 vn, bc	D-Hs, GB-Lbm, *Lbm[R], Thomas Coram Foundation, London, Och. T. US-Cu, NBu	related to Chapel Royal settings	xxxiv, 207	
Have mercy upon me. O God (3), c	S, T, STB, ob, bn, 2 vn, bc	D-Hs, M. Schou's private collection, Denmark. GB-BENcoke. H. Lbm. *Lbm[R], Thomas Coram Foundation, London, US-Cu, NBu		xxxiv, 79	
In the Lord put I my trust (2), d	T. STB, ob, bn, 2 vn, bc	D-Hs, GB-BENcoke, Cfm, Lbm, *Lbm[R], US-Cu	see 'Keyboard': 206	xxxiv, 3	
I will magnify thee, O God (5A), A	S, T, STB, ob, bn, 2 vn. bc	D-Hs, GB-BENcoke, Lbm, *Lbm[R], Lcm. Ob. T. US-Cu, NBu	movts The Lord is righteous and Happy, happy are addns; see Beeks (1978)	xxxiv, 133	
Let God arise (11A), Bb	S, T, SATB, ob, bn, 2 vn. bc	D-Hs, GB-Lbm, *Lbm[R], Lcm, T, US-Cu, NBu		xxxv, 211	34
My song shall be alway (7), G	S, A, T, B, SATB, ob, bn, 2 vn, bc	GB-Cfm, DRc, Lbm, *Lbm[R], T. US-Cu, NBu	Thou rulest the raging of the sea (trio), in Arnold's edn. (London, 1783), may be spurious; see Beeks (1978)	xxxv, 1	

Title	Scoring	Sources	Remarks	Edition
O be joyful ('Chandos' Jubilate) (1), D	S, T, B, STB, ob, bn, 2 vn, bc	GB-Cfm, H, Lbm, *Lbm[R], Thomas Coram Foundation, London, Ob, US-Cu	arr. of 'Utrecht' Jubilate	xxxiv, 1
O come let us sing unto the Lord (8), A	S, 2 T, STTB, ob, bn, 2 rec, 2 vn, bc	D-Hs, GB-Cfm, DRc, Lbm, *Lbm[R], Lcm, Mp, US-Cu, NBu		xxxv, 41
O praise the Lord with one consent (9), Eb	S, 2 T, B, STTB, ob, 2 vn, bc	D-Hs, GB-BENcoke, *Cfm, DRc, GL, H, Lbm, Lbm[R], Lgc, T, US-Cu, NBu		xxxv, 98
O sing unto the Lord (4), F	S, T, STB, ob, bn, 2 vn, bc	D-Hs, M. Schou's private collection, Denmark, GB-Cfm, DRc, Lbm, *Lbm[R], Thomas Coram Foundation, London, Mp, US-Cu, NBu	partly based on Chapel Royal setting	xxxiv, 109
The Lord is my light (10), g	S, 2 T, STTTB, 2 rec, ob, 2 vn, bc	D-Hs, GB-BENcoke, Cfm, Lbm, *Lbm[R]. Mp, Och, T, US-Cu		xxxv, 151
Coronation anthems:		D-Hs, GB-Cfm, H, *Lbm[R], Lcm, Mp	for coronation of George II; perf. Westminster Abbey, 11 Oct 1727	xiv [iii/8] 34
Let thy hand be strengthened, G	SAATB, 2 ob, [bn], str, bc			
My heart is inditing, D	SAATBB, 2 ob, [bn], 3 tpt, timp, str, bc			
The king shall rejoice, D	SAATBB, 2 ob, bn, 3 tpt, timp, str, bc			
Zadok the priest, D	SSAATBB, 2 ob, 2 bn, 3 tpt, timp, str, bc			
Other occasional anthems: As pants the hart (6C), d	S, 2 A, 2 B, SAATBB, org, viol/vc	*Lbm, Ob, US-NBu	mainly for Chapel Royal Chapel Royal, 1711–14	xxxiv, 277
As pants the hart (6D), d	S, 2 A, 2 B, SAATBB, viol/vc, org	*GB-Lbm[R]	for Chapel Royal, 1722–6; rev. of above	xxxvi, 233
As pants the hart (6B), d	S, 2 A, T, 2 B, SAATBB, ob[1738: 2 ob], str, bc	††GB-Lbm, *Lbm[R], US-Cu, NBu	1722–6, ? perf. Chapel Royal, 7 Oct 1722, related to Chandos and above versions; new setting of Now when I think … For I went with the multitude, and Allelujah (from Athalia) added for 'An Oratorio', 28 March 1738	xxxiv, 239

Title/first words, Key	Scoring	MS sources	Remarks	HG	HHA
Blessed are they that consider the poor ('Foundling Hospital Anthem') (16), d	2 S, A, T, SATB, 2 ob, 2 tpt, timp, str, bc	Lbm, *Lbm[R], †Thomas Coram Foundation, London, T, US-NBu	perf. Foundling Hospital, 27 May 1749; music partly from Funeral Anthem, Susanna and Messiah	xxxvi, 154	—
How beautiful are the feet ('Anthem on the Peace'), d	S, 2 A, T, B, SATB, fl, ob, bn, 2 tpt, timp, str, bc	*GB-Lbm[R]	for Peace of Aix-la-Chapelle; perf. Chapel Royal, 25 April 1749; music arr. from I will magnify (Chapel Royal setting), Occasional Oratorio and Messiah; see Burrows (1973): facs. of 1st chorus in Das Autograph des Oratoriums 'Messias', ed. F. Chrysander (Hamburg, 1892/R), 285; ed. D. Burrows as The Anthem on the Peace (London, 1981)	—	
I will magnify Thee, O God (5B), A	A, T, B, SATB, ob, str, bc	EIRE-Dmh, GB-Lbm, *Lbm[R], Mp, US-Cu, NBu	1722–6; ? perf. Chapel Royal, 5 Jan 1724; based on movts from 4 Chandos anthems	xxxiv, 169	
Let God arise (11B), A	A, B, SATB, ob, bn, str, bc	GB-BENcoke, Cfm, Lbm, *Lbm[R], Mp, US-NBu	1722–6; ? perf. Chapel Royal, 16 Jan 1726; partly based on Chandos setting	xxxv, 263	
O sing unto the Lord (4A), G	A, B, SATB, fl, 2 ob, 2 tpt, str	*GB-Lbm[R]	1712–14; ? perf. Chapel Royal, 26 Sept 1714	xxxvi, 219	
Sing unto God (14), D	S, A, T, B, SATB, 2 ob, 2 tpt, ? timp, str, bc	D-Hs, *GB-Cfm, DRc, Lbm[R], T, US-NBu	for wedding of Prince Frederick and Princess Augusta of Saxe-Coburg; perf. Chapel Royal, 27 April 1736; final movt from Il Parnasso in festa: re-used, with addns from This is the day, for wedding of Prince Frederick of Hesse and Princess Mary, Chapel Royal, 8 May 1740	xxxvi, 80	
The king shall rejoice ('Dettingen Anthem') (15), D	A, B, SSATB, 2 ob, bn, 3 tpt, timp, str, bc	D-Hs, GB-BENcoke, DRc, *Lbm, Mp, J-Tn, US-NBu	for victory at Dettingen; completed 3 Aug 1743; perf. Chapel Royal, 27 Nov 1743 with 'Dettingen' Te Deum	xxxvi, 111	

Title	Forces	Sources	Remarks		
The ways of Zion do mourn ('Funeral Anthem'), g	SSATB, 2 ob, 2 bn, str, bc	GB-Cfm, DRc, Lbm, *Lbm[R], Mp	for funeral of Queen Caroline; completed 12 Dec 1737; perf. Westminster Abbey, 17 Dec 1737; used with altered words as pt.i of Israel in Egypt, 1739	xi	[iii/9]
This is the day (13), D	A, T, B, SSAATTBB, 2 fl, 2 ob, bn, 2 tpt, ? timp, str, bc	†D-Hs	for wedding of Princess Anne and Prince William of Orange; perf. German Chapel, St James's, 14 March 1734; music mainly from Athalia; see Sing unto God	xxxvi, 27	
Liturgical settings:					
Te Deum, 'Utrecht', D	2 S, 2 A, T, B, SSAATB, fl, 2 ob, 2 tpt. str, bc	D-Hs, GB-BENcoke, Cfm, DRc, Lbm, *Lbm[R], Mp	for Peace of Utrecht; completed 14 Jan 1713; perf. St Paul's, 7 July 1713	xxxi, 2	[iii/4] 18, 57
Jubilate, 'Utrecht', D	2 A, B, SSAATTBB, 2 ob, 2 tpt, str, bc	D-Hs, GB-BENcoke, Cfm, DRc, Lbm, *Lbm[R], Mp	for Peace of Utrecht; perf. St Paul's, 7 July 1713; late arr. as O be joyful	xxxi, 46	[iii/4] 24
Jubilate, 'Chandos', D			see O be joyful		
Te Deum, 'Caroline', D	2 A, T, B, SAATB, fl, ? 2 tpt, str	*Cfm, Lbm, *Lbm[R], Mp, Ob	? perf. Chapel Royal, 26 Sept 1714; rev. with new version of Vouchsafe, O Lord, 1722–6, repeated 25 April 1749; later perfs. probably with 2 ob	xxxvii, 1	19
Te Deum, 'Chandos', Bb	S, 2 T, B, STTTB, fl, ob, bn, tpt, str, bc	D-Hs, GB-Cfm, Lbm, *Lbm[R], Mp, US-NBu	c1718, for James Brydges, later Duke of Chandos	xxxvii, 25	24, 99
Te Deum, A	A, T, 2 B, SAATBB, fl, ob, bn, str, bc	M. Schou's private collection, Denmark, GB-BENcoke, Lbm, *Lbm[R], Lcm, Mp, US-NBu	1722–6; ? perf. Chapel Royal, 16 Jan 1726, based on 'Chandos' Te Deum	xxxvii, 109	
Te Deum, 'Dettingen', D	2 S, A, T, B, SSATB, 2 ob, bn, 3 tpt, timp, str, bc	GB-BENcoke, DRc, Lcm, *Lbm[R], Lsp, Lwa, Mp, US-CA	for victory at Dettingen; perf. Chapel Royal, 27 Nov 1743	xxv	[iii/5] 57
Spurious:					
O praise the Lord, ye angels of his (12)			probably by M. Greene; see Johnstone (1976)	xxvi, 1	
Behold, now is the acceptable time			edn. (Hilversum, 1964); arr. of solo, The righteous Lord, from In the Lord put I my trust	—	

Italian sacred cantatas

First words (Title)	Scoring	MS sources	Remarks	HG	HHA
Ah, che troppo ineguali	S, str, bc	*GB-Lbm[R]		liiB, 148	
Donna che in ciel	S, SATB, str, bc	D-MÜs	cantata for BVM; ?frag. for anniversary of deliverance of Rome from earthquake; ? perf. Rome, c2 Feb 1707; ed. R. Ewerhart (Cologne, 1959)	—	
Giunta l'ora fatal (Il pianto di Maria)	S, 4 vn, va, bc	MÜs, GB-Lbm, I-PAc, Rsc, Sac	attrib. Handel in MSS and in document of 1711 (see Fabbri, 1964), but doubtful on stylistic grounds	—	9

German sacred music

German church cantatas, presumably composed at Halle before 1704, are no longer extant; see Serauky (1940), 70ff, for text incipits of 7 lost cantatas attrib. Handel. The St John Passion (HG ix, HHA i/2), the cantata Ach Herr, mich armer Sünder (ed. M. Seiffert, Leipzig, 1928) and other unpublished works are almost certainly spurious; see Chrysander (1858–67), i, 64–70, W. Braun, HJb 1959, and Händel-Ehrung (1959). For Brockes Passion, see 'Oratorios'.   4

SECULAR CANTATAS
Dramatic cantatas

First words (Title)	Scoring	MS sources	Remarks	HG	HHA
Amarilli vezzosa (Il duello amoroso)	S, A, 2 vn, bc	D-MÜs	copyist's bill: 28 Aug 1708	—	
Arresta il passo (Aminta e Fillide)	2 S, 3 vn, va, bc	MÜs, *GB-Lbm[R]	perf. 14 July 1708	liiA, 21	8
Chi ben ama	2 S, str, bc	D-MÜs, *GB-Lbm[R]	frag. added to Arresta il passo	liiB, 140	
Cor fedele (Clori, Tirsi e Fileno)	2 S, A, 2 rec, 2 ob, str, archlute, bc	D-MÜs, *GB-Lbm[R]	copyist's bill: 10 Oct 1707; HG prints only frag. extant in autograph; ov. used for Oreste c1708	liiB, 99	
La terra è liberata (Apollo e Dafne)	S, B, fl, 2 ob, bn, str, bc	*Lbm[R]		liiB, 1	11, 12
O come chiare e belle (Olinto, Il Tebro, Gloria)	2 S, A, tpt, 2 vn, bc	D-MÜs, *GB-Lbm[R]	copyist's bill: 10 Sept 1708	liiB, 38	8
Sorge il dì (Aci, Galatea e Polifemo)	S, A, B, 2 rec, ob, 2 tpt, 2 vn, va, 2 vc, bc	*Lbm, *Lbm[R]	completed 16 June 1708	liii	[i/5] 9, 11, 12, 29

[Cantata per Carlo VI]	3 S, A, B, 2 rec, 2 ob, str, bc	*Lbm[R]	c1710, inc.; opening and title not known; frags. in HG do not incl. all extant material	iiB, 47

Solo and duo cantatas with instruments

Title	Scoring	Sources	Notes	Ref.
Ah! crudel nel pianto mio	S, 2 ob, str, bc	*D-MÜs, GB-Lbm[R]	c1707	iiiA, 1
Alla caccia (Diana cacciatrice)	S, coro (unison S), tpt, 2 vn, bc	*A-Wgm, *D-Bds	copyist's bill: 16 May 1707	
Alpestre monte	S, 2 vn, bc	*GB-Lbm[R], Mp, Ob	HG prints only frag. extant in autograph	iiiA, 17
Behold, where Venus weeping stands (Venus and Adonis) (J. Hughes)	S, ?vn, bc	Lbm	c1711; only 2 airs extant in kbd transcr. Dear Adonis and Transporting Joy, separately ed. W. C. Smith and H. Brian (London, 1938)	—
Carco sempre di gloria	A, str, bc	*Lbm[R]	? for Annibali, March 1737: arr. from Cecilia, volgi un sguardo, with new aria; bc acc. only in HG	iiiA, 96
Cecilia, volgi un sguardo	S, T, str, bc	*Lbm[R]	perf. King's Theatre, Haymarket, London, Feb 1736	iiiA, 78
Clori, mia bella Clori	S, str, bc	D-MÜs, *GB-Lbm[R]		iiiA, 107
Crudel tiranno amor	S, str, bc	D-LEm, GB-Cfm, Lam, Ob	? perf. King's Theatre, 5 July 1721: all 3 arias added to Floridante, Dec 1722	iiiA, 113
Cuopre tal volta	B, 2 vn, bc	D-MÜs, *GB-Lbm[R]		iiiA, 121
Da quel giorno fatale (Il delirio amoroso)	S, rec, 3 vn, va, vc, bc	D-Hs, MÜs, GB-Lbm[R]	copyist's bill: 14 May 1707	iiiA, 130
Dietro l'orme fuggaci (Armida abbandonata)	S, 2 vn, bc	D-MÜs, *GB-Lbm[R]	copyist's bill: 30 June 1707	iiiA, 153
Dunque sarà pur vero (Agrippina condotta a morire)	S, 2 vn, bc	D-MÜs, *GB-Lbm[R]	c1708	iiiA, 162
Figlio d'alte speranze	S, vn, bc	*Lbm[R]		iiiA, 174; iiB, 156
Languia di bocca lusinghiera	S, ob, vn, bc	*US-NYp		iiiA, 101, 23, 80
[Look down, harmonious Saint] (N. Hamilton: The Power of Musick)	T, str, bc	*GB-Lbm[R]	frag. ?1736: ? written for Alexander's Feast, incl. instead in Cecilia, volgi un sguardo	
Mi palpita il cor	i: S, ob, bc; ii: A, fl, bc; iii: A, fl/ob, bc	i: *GB-Lbm[R]; ii: D-Hs, GB-Cfm, *Lbm[R], Lbm, Mp, Ob; iii: *GB-Cfm, Lbm[R], Lbm, Ob	for further versions see continuo cantatas Mi palpita and Dimmi, o mio cor	iiB, 152 (i); 1, 153 (ii)

8, 11

First words (Title)	Scoring	MS sources	Remarks	HG	HHA
Nel dolce dell'oblio (Pensieri notturni di Filli)	S, rec, bc	*Lbm[R]		liiB, 30	
No se emenderá jamás (Cantata spagnuola)	S, gui, bc	†D-MÜs, *GB-Lbm[R]	copyist's bill: 22 Sept 1707; autograph of version of final aria sold Sotheby's, London, 13 April 1954 (facs. in catalogue)	liiB, 34	
Notte placida e cheta	S, 2 vn, bc	D-MÜs		—	
Qual ti riveggio, oh Dio	S, 2 ob, str, bc	*G. Flörsheim's private collection, Basle, *US-NYpm	? copyist's bill: 28 Aug 1708 see Kinsky (1953) 1–4, and Marx (1976)	—	
Spande ancor	B, 2 vn, bc	*GB-Lbm[R]		liiB, 60	
Splende l'alba in oriente	A, 2 ?fl, ob, str, bc	*Lbm[R]		liiA, 69	
Tra le fiamme	S, 2 rec, 2 vn, va da gamba, bc	D-MÜs, *GB-Lbm[R], Ob		liiB, 66	
Tu fedel? tu costante?	S, 2 vn, bc	D-MÜs, *GB-Lbm[R]	copyist's bill: 16 May 1707	liiB, 79	
Un alma innamorata	S, vn, bc	D-MÜs, *GB-Lbm[R], T	copyist's bill: 30 June 1707	liiB, 92	
		Solo cantatas with basso continuo			
Ah, che pur troppo è vero	S	GB-Lbm, *Lbm[R], Lcm, Mp		I, 1	
Allor ch'io dissi	S	Cfm, Lbm, *Lbm[R], Lcm, Mp		I, 8	
Aure soavi e liete	S	†D-MÜs, GB-Cfm, Lbm, *Lbm[R], Lcm, Mp, Ob	copyist's bill: 16 May 1707	I, 12	
Bella ma ritrosetta	S	*Cfm, Ob		—	
Care selve	S	D-MÜs, GB-Lbm, *Lbm[R], Lcm, Mp, Ob		I, 16	
Chi rapì la pace	S	D-MÜs, GB-Lbm, *Lbm[R], Lcm, Mp, Ob	copyist's bill: 31 Aug 1709	I, 20	
Clori, degli occhi miei	A	Lbm, *Lbm[R], Lcm, Mp, Ob		I, 24	
Clori, ove sei	S	Lbm, Lcm, Mp, Ob		I, 30	
Clori, si ch'io t'adoro	S	Mp		—	
Clori, vezzosa Clori	S	D-MÜs	copyist's bill: 9 Aug 1708	—	
Dal fatale momento	i: S; ii: B	i: GB-Lbm, Mp; iii: D-LEm		I, 34 (i)	
Dalla guerra amorosa	i: B; ii: S	i: GB-Lbm, Lbm[R], Lcm; iii: D-MÜs	copyist's bill: 31 Aug 1709	I, 39	
Da sete ardente afflitto	S	Hs, MÜs, GB-Cfm, CDp, Lbm, Lcm, Mp, Ob	copyist's bill: 31 Aug 1709		

Title	Voice	Sources	Notes	Page
Deh! lasciate e vita e volo	A	*Ob	text partly P. A. Rolli: Di canzonette e di cantate (London, 1727), no.22	l. 44
Del bel idolo mio	S	D-MÜs, GB-Lbm, *Lbm[R], Lcm, Mp, Ob	copyist's bill: 31 Aug 1709	l. 48
Dimmi, o mio cor	S	Lbm, *Lbm[R], Ob	similar to conclusion of Mi palpita il cor	l. 53
Dite, miè piante	S	D-MÜs, GB-Cfm, Lbm, Lcm, Mp, Ob	copyist's bill: 9 Aug 1708	l. 58
Dolce pur d'amor l'affanno	i: A; ii: S	i: *Cfm, Lbm, Lcm, Mp, Ob; ii: D-Hs	last aria also in Stanco di più soffrire	l. 68 (i), 72 (ii)
E partirai, mia vita?	i: S; ii: S	i: Hs, GB-Cfm, Lbm, *Lbm[R], Lcm, Mp, Ob; ii: *Lbm[R] Lbm, Lbm[R], Lcm, Ob		l. 76 (i), 81 (ii)
Figli del mesto cor	A	D-MÜs, GB-Lbm, *Lbm[R], Lcm, Mp, Ob		l. 86
Filli adorata e cara	S		copyist's bill: 31 Aug 1709	l. 90
Fra pensieri quel pensiero	A	D-MÜs, *GB-Cfm, Lcm, Ob	copyist's bill: 31 Aug 1709	l. 94
Fra tante pene	S	D-MÜs, GB-Lbm, *Lbm[R]	copyist's bill: 9 Aug 1708	l. 98
Hendel, non può mia musa	S	*D-MÜs, GB-Cfm, Lbm, Mp	text in Rolli: Di canzonette e di cantate (1727), no.3: autograph of final aria (È troppo bella) sold Sotheby's, London. May 1917, facs. in Maggs Bros. Catalogue 362 (London, 1917), plate V; ed. W. H. Cummings as La bella pastorella (London, c1887)	—
[H]o fuggito amore	A	*Ob		l. 171
Irene, idolo mio	i: S; ii: A	i: D-MÜs, GB-Cfm; ii: Lcm, Mp, Ob		l. 102 (ii)
L'aure grate, il fresco rio (La solitudine)	i: S; ii: A	i: Cfm, *Lbm[R]; ii: CDp, Ob	i, unfinished: ii, c1718: see Boyd (1968); ed. M. Boyd (Kassel, 1970)	l. 107 (i) —
Lungi dal mio bel nume	S	i: D-Hs, MÜs, GB-Cfm, CDp, *Lbm, Lcm, Ob; ii: *Lbm[R], Lbm	i, completed Rome, 3 March 1708	l. 110 (i), 117 (ii)
Lungi da me pensier tiranno	i: S; ii: A	i: D-MÜs, GB-Cfm, Mp; ii: Lcm, Mp, Ob	copyist's bill: 31 Aug 1709	l. 122(ii)
Lungi da voi, che siete poli	i: S; ii: A	i: D-MÜs; ii: GB-Lcm, Mp	copyist's bill: 9 Aug 1708	l. 128 (ii)
Lungi n'andò Fileno	S	Cfm, Lbm, *Lbm[R], Lcm, Mp; Ob	copyist's bill: 28 Aug 1708	l. 134
Manca pur quanto sai	S	D-MÜs, GB-CDp, Lbm, *Lbm[R], Mp, Ob	copyist's bill: 9 Aug 1708	l. 140

First words (Title)	Scoring	MS sources	Remarks	HG	HHA
Mentre il tutto è in furore	S	D-MÜs, GB-Lcm	copyist's bill: 28 Aug 1708; autograph sold Sotheby's, London, 18 Feb 1963; GB-Lbm, facs. suppl. x, ff.116-21	I, 144	
Menzognere speranze	S	D-MÜs, GB-Lbm[R], Lbm, Lcm, Mp, Ob	copyist's bill: 22 Sept 1707	I, 149	
Mi palpita il cor	S	D-Hs, *GB-Cfm, Lcm, Mp, Ob	Cfm 252, 5-6 has 1 aria for A; cf Mi palpita ('Solo and duo cantatas with instruments') and Dimmi, o mio cor	I, 161	
Nel dolce tempo	i: A; ii: S	i: Lbm, Mp, Ob; ii: D-MÜs, GB-Lcm		I, 166 (i)	
Nell' africane selve	B	i: Lbm, *Lbm[R], Ob; ii: Cfm		I, 172 (i)	
Nella stagion, che di viole	i: S; ii: A	i: D-MÜs, GB-Lbm, Lbm[R], Lcm, Mp; ii: Cfm	copyist's bill: 16 May 1707	I, 178 (i)	
Ne' tuoi lumi, o bella Clori	S	D-Hs, MÜs, GB-Cfm, Lbm, Lcm, Mp, Ob	copyist's bill: 22 Sept 1707	I, 182	
Nice che fa? che pensa?	S	Lbm, *Lbm[R], Lcm, Mp		II, 1	
Ninfe e pastori	i: S; ii: A; iii: S	i: D-MÜs, GB-Cfm. *Lbm[R] Lcm; ii: Lbm[R]; iii: *Lbm[R], Mp, Ob	copyist's bill: 28 Feb 1709	II, 6 (i), 11 (ii), 16 (iii)	
Non sospirar, non piangere	S	Lbm, *Lbm[R], Lcm		II, 20	
Occhi miei. che faceste?	S	D-Hs, MÜs, GB-Lbm, *Lbm[R], Lcm, Mp, Ob		II, 24	
O lucenti, o sereni occhi	S	D-MÜs, GB-Lbm, Lbm[R], Lcm, Mp, Ob		II, 28	
O numi eterni (La Lucrezia)	S	D-MÜs, GB-Cfm, Lbm, *Lbm[R], Lcm, Mp, Ob	copyist's bill: 31 Aug 1709	II, 32	
Parti, l'idolo mio	S	Lbm, Lcm		II, 43	
Poichè giuraro amore	S	D-MÜs, GB-Lbm, *Lbm[R], Lcm, Mp, Ob	copyist's bill: 16 May 1707	II, 48	
Qualor crudele si mia vaga Dori	A	CDp, Lbm, Lcm, Mp, Ob		II, 53	
Qualor l'egre pupille	S	D-MÜs, GB-Cfm, Lbm, Lcm, Mp, Ob	copyist's bill: 22 Sept 1707	II, 59	
Qual sento io non conosciuto	S	Mp		—	
Quando sperasti, o core	i: S; ii: A	i: D-Hs, MÜs, GB-Cfm, Lbm, *Lbm[R], Lcm, Mp; ii: Ob	copyist's bill: 9 Aug 1708	II, 64 (i)	
Quel fior che all'alba ride	S	*Cfm	c1739; also set as trio and duet	—	

Sans y penser			see 'Songs and hymns'	
Sarai contenta un di	S	*D-Hs, MÜs, GB-Lbm,* *Lbm[R], Lcm, Mp*		ii, 68
Sarei troppo felice	S	*D-Hs, MÜs, GB-Cfm, Lbm, Lcm, Mp, Ob*	copyist's bill: 22 Sept 1707	ii, 72 (without final recits and aria)
Sei pur bella, pur vezzosa (La bianca rosa)	S	i: *D-MÜs, GB-Lbm, *Lbm[R], Lcm, Ob;* ii: *Lbm[R];* iii: *D-Hs, *GB-Lbm[R], Mp*	copyist's bill: 16 May 1707; ii ? not by Handel, but used by him in i and iii	ii, 76 (i), 80 (ii), 86 (iii)
Sento là che ristretto	i: A; ii: S; iii: S	i: *Lbm, *Lbm[R], Mp, Ob;* ii: *D-MÜs, GB-Cfm, Lbm;* iii: *D-Hs, *GB-Lbm[R], Mp, Ob*	copyist's bill: 31 Aug 1709; ii is i transposed	ii, 90 (i), 96 (iii)
Se pari è la tua fe	S	i: *Lbm, *Lbm[R], Lcm, Mp;* ii: †*D-MÜs;* iii: *GB-Cfm, Lcm, Mp, Ob*	copyist's bill for ii: 28 Aug 1708	ii, 102 (i), 106 (iii)
Se per fatal destino	S	*D-Hs, MÜs, GB-Lbm, *Lbm[R], Lcm, Mp*	copyist's bill: 16 May 1707	ii, 111
Siete rose rugiadose	A	†*Cfm, CDp, Lbm, *Lbm[R], Ob*		ii, 115
S'il ne falloit (Cantate françoise)			see 'Songs and hymns'	
Solitudini care, amata libertà	S	*Cfm, Lcm, Mp*		ii, 118
Son gelsomino (Il gelsomino)	i: S; ii: A	i: *D-Hs, GB-Cfm, Lbm, *Lbm[R], Lcm, Mp, Ob;* iii: *Cfm, Lbm, Ob*	text in Rolli: Di canzonette e di cantate (1727), no.17	ii, 125 (i)
Stanco di più soffrire	i: A; ii: S	i: *Cfm, Lbm, Lcm, Mp, Ob;* ii: *D-MÜs*	copyist's bill for ii: 9 Aug 1708; last aria also in Dolce pur d'amor l'affanno	ii, 130 (i)
Stelle, perfide stelle (Partenza di G. B.)	S	*Hs, MÜs, GB-Cfm, CDp, Lbm, *Lbm[R], Lcm, Mp, Ob*	1707	ii, 134
Torna il core al suo diletto	S	*D-MÜs, GB-Lcm, Mp*	HG erroneously incl. aria Allor che sorge; copyist's bill for ii: 16 May 1707	ii, 138
Udite il mio consiglio	S	i: *Lbm[R], Lcm;* ii: †*D-MÜs*		ii, 143
Un sospir a chi si muove	S	*GB-Lbm, *Lbm[R], Lcm, Mp*	in some MSS incl. as part of Venne voglia, but autographs headed separately	ii, 153
Vedendo amor	A	*Cfm, Lbm, *Lbm[R], Lcm*		ii, 158
Venne voglia ad amore	A	*Cfm, Lbm, *Lbm[R], Lcm*	cantata Amore uccellatore, *Cfm,* incl. Venne voglia, Vedendo amor and other new material	ii, 164

First words (Title)	Scoring	MS sources	Remarks	HG	HHA
Zeffiretto, arresta il volo	S	Lbm, *Lbm[R], Lcm, Mp	copyist's bill for final aria: 31 Aug 1709	ii, 168	

The aria Sposo ingrato from Radamisto is stated by Burney (BurneyH, iv, 261; ii, 702) as originally being from the cantata Casti amori (? in his collection); he also mentioned (1785, 'Sketch', p.[*7], fn (a)) MS of 2 cantatas 'which I never saw elsewhere', one with hpd obbl.

Lamarciata is listed among Handel cantatas in copyist's bill, 9 Aug 1708; see Kirkendale (1967), 165, document 24.

On 6 Feb 1711 (Queen Anne's birthday) 'a Dialogue in Italian, in Her Majesty's Praise, set … by … Mr. Hendel' was perf. at St James's Palace, London; reported in The Political State of Great Britain, i(1711), 227.

Unidentified cantatas

Doubtful and spurious cantatas

First words (Title)	Scoring	MS sources	Remarks	HG	HHA
Dalle tenebre orrende (Orfeo ed. Euridice)	2 S, bc	D-MÜs, GB-Lbm	attrib. J. A. Hasse in other MSS	—	
Dolce mio ben	S, bc	Lcm 257, ff.28–32	late insertion into Lcm MS, not attrib. Handel	1, 62	
Lilla, vedi quel colle	A, bc	Lbm Add.14182, ff.78–80	attrib. Telemann in D-DS and DK-Kk: ed. M. Seiffert (Cologne, 1935); see W. Menke: Das Vokalwerk Georg Philipp Telemanns (Kassel, 1942), 125, and R. Donington: 'Amore traditore: a Problem Cantata', Studies in Eighteenth-century Music: a Tribute to Karl Geiringer (New York and London, 1970), 171f. 176n	—	
Pastorella vaga bella	S, hpd, b	D-DS, LEm, DK-Kk			
Selve caverne e monti	S, bc	D-MÜs, GB-Lbm	GB-Lbm Add.14165, f.83, attrib. D. Scarlatti		
Usignuol che tra le fronde	S, bc	Lbm Add.14207, ff.180–85	dialogue cantatas arr. (? by W. Hayes) from items in Ottone, Flavio and Giulio Cesare; duet Gentle Hymen is arr. of Non tardate a festeggiar (Ottone addition, 1733); rest of music identified in Zanetti (1959)		
3 English cantatas	1: S, T; 2: S, Bar; 3: T, Bar; all with 2 vn. bc	Ob (score), I-Rsc (parts, lacking vn 1)			
1 To lonely shades fair Delia stray'd					
2 With roving and ranging					
3 So pleasing the pain is					

Index of cantata titles: Aci, Galatea e Polifemo (dramatic: Sorge il dì); Agrippina condotta a morire (solo … with insts: Dunque sarà pur vero); Aminta e Fillide (dramatic: Arresta il passo); Amore uccellatore (solo with bc: Venne voglia ad amore); Apollo e Dafne (dramatic: La terra è liberata); Armida abbandonata (solo … with insts: Dietro l'orme fuggaci); Bianca rosa (solo with bc: Sei pur bella); Cantata spagnuola (solo … with insts: No se emenderà jamás); Cantate françoise (see 'Songs and hymns'); Clori, Tirsi e Fileno (dramatic: Cor fedele); Diana cacciatrice (solo … with insts: Alla caccia); Delirio amoroso (solo … with insts: Da quel giorno fatale); Duello amoroso (dramatic: Amarilli vezzosa); Ero e Leandro (unauthentic title) (solo … with insts: Qual ti riveggio); Gelsomino (solo with bc: Son gelsomino); Lucrezia (solo- with bc: O numi eterni); Olinto, Il Tebro, Gloria (dramatic: O come chiare e belle); Orfeo ed Euridice (spurious: Dalle tenebre orrende); Partenza di G.B (solo with bc: Stelle, perfide stelle); Pensieri notturni di Filli (solo with insts: Nel dolce dell'oblio); Solitudine (solo with bc: L'aure grate); Tebro (see Olinto, Il Tebro, Gloria); Venus and Adonis (solo … with insts: Behold where Venus)

DUETS AND TRIOS WITH CONTINUO
(references to HG xxxii are to enlarged 2/1880)

First words (Title)	Scoring	MS sources	Remarks	HG	HHA
Ahi, nelle sorte umane	2 S	GB-BENcoke, *Lbm[R]	completed 31 Aug 1745	xxxii, 152	
A miravi io son intento	S, A	D-Hs, MÜs, GB-BENcoke, *Cfm, Lbm, Lbm[R], J-Tn, US-NBu	by 1710–11	xxxii, 68	
Amor gioje mi porge	2 S	D-Hs, MÜs, GB-BENcoke, *Cfm, Lbm, Lbm[R], US-NBu	by 1710–11	xxxii, 52	
Beato in ver che può (after Horace: Beatus ille)	S, A	GB-BENcoke, *Lbm[R]	completed 31 Oct 1742	xxxii, 138	
Caro autor di mia doglia	i: S, T; ii: 2 S; iii: 2 A	ii: Cfm, *Lbm[R]; iii: D-Hs, MÜs, GB-BENcoke, US-NBu; iii: GB-Lbm, *Lbm[R]	i, c1707; ii, in R. Keiser: Divertimenti serenissimi (Hamburg, 1713), but probably by Handel; iii, c1735 40, final movt inc.	xxxii, 18 / xxxii, 10	
Che vai pensando	S, B	D-Hs, MÜs, GB-BENcoke, *Cfm, Lbm, Lbm[R], J-Tn, US-NBu	by 1710–11	xxxii, 45	
Conservate, raddoppiate	S, A	D-Hs, MÜs, GB-BENcoke, *Cfm, Lbm, Lbm[R], US-NBu	by 1710–11	xxxii, 89	
Fronda leggiera e mobile	S, A	GB-BENcoke, *Lbm[R]	c1744	xxxii, 144	
Giù nei tartarei regni	S, B	Cfm, *Lbm[R]	c1707–9	xxxii, 24	
Langue, geme e sospira	S, A	D-Hs, MÜs, GB-BENcoke, Cfm, *Lbm[R], US-NBu	?1711: text in G. D. de Totis: La caduta del regno dell'Amazzoni (Rome, 1690)	xxxii, 102	
No, di voi non vuo fidarmi	i: 2 S; ii: S, A	i: GB-BENcoke, *Lbm[R]; ii: *Lbm[R]	i completed 3 July 1741; ii completed 2 Nov 1742	xxxii, 122 (i), 130 (ii)	

First words (Title)	Scoring	MS sources	Remarks	HG	HHA
Quando in calma ride il mare	S. B	D-Hs, MÜs, GB-BENcoke, *Cfm, Lbm[R], US-NBu GB-Cfm, Lbm	by 1710–11	xxxii, 75	
Quel fior ch'all'alba nasce	2 S. B	D-Hs, GB-BENcoke, Cfm, Lbm, Lbm[R], US-NBu	?c1708; similar to above item; also as solo cantata and duet		
Quel fior ch'all'alba ride	2 S. B			xxxii, 166	
Quel fior ch'all'alba ride	2 S	GB-BENcoke, *Lbm[R]	completed 1 July 1741	xxxii, 116	
Se tu non lasci amore	2 S. B	i: D-Hs, MÜs, GB-BENcoke, Cfm, Lbm, Lbm[R], US-NBu; ii: *G. Flörsheim's private collection, Basle, GB-Cfm	ii, completed 12 July 1708, has extended 1st movt; see W. H. Cummings' note in MA, iii (1911), 59–60, and Kinsky (1953), 4 – 6	xxxii, 158	
Se tu non lasci amore	S. A	BENcoke, Cfm, *Lbm[R], US-NBu	?1711	xxxii, 108	
Sono liete, fortunate	S. A	*D-Bds, Hs, MÜs, GB-BENcoke, *Cfm, Lbm, Lbm[R], US-NBu	by 1710–11	xxxii, 31	
Tacete, ohime, tacete	S. B	D-Hs, MÜs, GB-BENcoke, *Cfm, Lbm, Lbm[R], US-NBu	by 1710–11; text by F. de Lemene (Poesia Diverse, Milan, 1694)	xxxii, 81	
Tanti strali al sen	S. A	D-Hs, MÜs, GB-BENcoke, *Cfm, Lbm, Lbm[R], US-NBu	by 1710–11	xxxii, 94	
Troppo cruda	S. A	*D-Bds, Hs, MÜs, GB-BENcoke, Lbm, Lbm[R], US-NBu	by 1710–11	xxxii, 36	
Va, speme infida	2 S	D-Hs, MÜs, GB-BENcokc, Cfm, Lbm, Lbm[R], J-Tn, US-NBu	by 1710–11; MS, ?autograph, sold White's, London, 1 March 1814	xxxii, 59	
		Spurious			
Cara sposa, io ti lascio	2 S		attrib. Handel in GB-Cfm 21, f.132r, attrib. A. Steffani in I-Vnm Cod.It.IV 768, f.27r; probably by neither		
Dalle tenebre orrende (Orfeo ed Euridice)	2 S		see 'Doubtful and spurious cantatas'		
Spero indarno	S. B		attrib. Handel in GB-Lbm Add. 5322, f.72r, doubtful		
When Phoebus the tops of the hills does adorn	S. A		see 'English songs'		

SONGS AND HYMNS

(unless otherwise indicated all for high voice and bc; none in HG or HHA)

The Monthly Mask of Vocal Music (London, new ser., 1717–24) [MM]
A General Collection of Minuets made for the Balls at Court . . . by Mr Handel (London, 1729) [incl. music only] [GCM, item no.]
A Choice Collection of English Songs set to Musick by Mr Handel (London, 1731) [CC, p. no.]

English songs

Published in contemporary songsheets and anthologies; few reliable MS sources known: details of printed sources in Smith (1960), 160–204.

First words (Title)	Text	Source	Remarks
As Celia's fatal arrows (The Unhappy Lovers)		CC, 1	probably authentic
As near Portobello lying (Hosier's Ghost)	R. Glover	The Muses' Delight (London, 1754), 190	spurious; see Come and listen
As on a sunshine summer's day	B. Griffin	GCM, 6	words added to probably authentic inst minuet; as 'Monsr Denoyer's Minuet' (Air XLIX) in C. Johnson: The Village Opera, Feb 1729, but as 'Handell's Minuet' (Air XX) in version of same work entitled The Chambermaid, Feb 1730
Ask not the cause (Charming Chloris)	J. Dryden	18th-century anthologies	words adapted to probably authentic music for another text; see The sun was sunk
Bacchus one day gaily striding (Bacchus' Speech in Praise of Wine)	T. Phillips	CC, 8; GCM, 35	words added to probably authentic inst minuet; tune is Air XVII in C. Coffey: The Devil to Pay, Aug 1731
Charming is your shape and air (The Polish Minuet, or Miss Kitty [The Reproof])		CC, 17; MM, Nov 1720	probably authentic; tune is Air V in G. Lillo: Sylvia, Nov 1730
Cloe proves false (The Slighted Swain)	A. Bradley	songsheet (c1720)	see Faithless, ungrateful
Come and listen (The Sailor's Complaint)		18th-century anthologies	spurious; for origins of tune see W. Chappell: *Old English Popular Music* (London, 1893), ii, 165; music not attrib. Handel until pubd as As near Portobello lying (see above)
Faithless, ungrateful (The Forsaken Maid's Complaint)		CC, 16; GCM, 30; MM, July 1722	words added to ?authentic inst minuet derived from No non piangete (Floridante); in anthologies as Cloe proves false (see above)
From scourging rebellion (A Song on the Victory obtained over the Rebels)	J. Lockman	songsheet (May 1746)	inst acc. indicated in the chorus
Guardian angels now protect me (The Forsaken Nymph [Leander])		songsheets (c1735–50); Amaryllis, ii (London, 1746), 64	probably spurious; not attrib. Handel until 1746 pubn

First words (Title)	Text	Source	Remarks
I like the amorous youth that's free	J. Miller: The Universal Passion	songsheet (c1737)	probably for 1st perf. of Miller's comedy, Drury Lane, 28 Feb 1737
Love's but the frailty of the mind	W. Congreve: The Way of the World	*GB-Cfm, Lbm[R]	perf. in revival of Congreve's play, Drury Lane, 17 March 1740; ed. A. H. Mann, Early English Musical Magazine i, no. 6 (June, 1891)
My fair, ye swains, is gone astray (Phillis)		Apollo's Cabinet (London, 1756), ii, 158	probably spurious
Not Cloe that I better am		British Musical Miscellany, v (London, 1736), 121	?authentic
Oh! cruel tyrant love (Strephon's Complaint of Love)		CC, 5	probably authentic; tune is Air XXV in J. Ralph: The Fashionable Lady, April 1730
Oh my dearest, my lovely creature		songsheet (c1719); MM, Dec 1719	words adapted to probably authentic music for another text; see Di godere ha speranza ('Italian songs')
On the shore of a low-ebbing sea (The Satyr's Advice to a Stock Jobber)		18th-century anthologies	words adapted to probably authentic music for another text; see Says my uncle
Phillis be kind	Parratt	British Musical Miscellany, ii (London, 1734), 10	words added to probably authentic inst minuet; as inst minuet in GB-Lbm[R] R.M.18.b.8. f.94r and Lbm Add.31467, f.31v; ed. in Pieces for the Harpsichord (London, 1928), no.70
Phyllis the lovely, turn to your Swain (Phillis Advised)		Bickham's Musical Entertainer (London, c1739), ii, 72	?authentic; not the same as Phillis the lovely, the charming and fair (to a minuet from the Water Music)
Says my uncle, I pray you discover (Molly Mog, or The Fair Maid of the Inn)	[J. Gay] Mist's Weekly Journal (27 Aug 1726)	CC, 14	probably authentic; in anthologies as On the shore of a low-ebbing sea (see above)
Stand round my brave boys (A Song made for the Gentleman Volunteers of the City of London)		songsheet (15 Nov 1745). *GB-Cfm (sketch)	perf. Drury Lane, 14 Nov 1745
The morning is charming (Hunting Song)	C. Legh	*Cfm (draft); *Adlington Hall, Cheshire (fair copy)	facs. of Adlington Hall MS in Streatfeild (1909), 304
The sun was sunk beneath the hill (The Poor [Despairing] Shepherd)	J. Gay	songsheet (c1725); CC, 13	probably authentic; in anthologies as Ask not the cause (see above)
'Twas when the seas were roaring (The Melancholy Nymph [The Faithful Maid])	Gay: The What d'ye call it (1715)	songsheet (c1725); CC, 24	probably authentic; ?orig. setting; tune is Air XXVIII in Gay: The Beggar's Opera, Jan 1728

First words (Title)			Remarks
Venus now leaves her Paphian dwelling		British Musical Miscellany, i (1734), 53	words added to probably authentic inst minuet; without attrib. as one of 3 'Songs ... on the Approaching Nuptial of the Prince of Orange'. March 1734: music = When I survey
When I survey Clarinda's charms (Matchless Clarinda [The Rapture])	'Mr. B'	songsheet (c1725); CC, 10; GCM, 23	words added to ?authentic inst minuet; attrib. Geminiani as kbd minuet in The Ladys Banquet, ii (May 1733), and as That which her slender waist confined, in Amaryllis, ii (1746); see Venus now leaves
When Phoebus the tops of the hills does adorn (A Hunting Song [The Death of the Stag])		songsheet (c1740)	?spurious; for S, A
Who to win a woman's favour	Cupid and Psyche, or Columbine Courtezan (1734)	Amaryllis, ii (1746), 55	words added to authentic inst minuet (related to minuet in Almira); as inst minuet in GB-Lbm[R] R.M. 18.b.8. f. 91v, and A-Wm XIV 743, f. 36r; ed. in Pieces for the Harpsichord (London, 1928), no. 66
Why will Florella when I gaze (Florella)	anon. in R. Steele: Poetical Miscellanies (London, 1714), 211	songsheet (c1725); CC, 9	?authentic; similar setting, in Amaryllis, ii (1746), attrib. W. Turner
Ye winds to whom Collin complains (An Answer to Collin's Complaint)		songsheet (c1720); CC, 27	probably authentic
Yes, I'm in love (The 'Je ne sa quoi')	W. Whitehead	songsheet (c1740); Amaryllis, ii (1746), 44	probably authentic

Many other Eng. songs using pre-existing music by Handel published in 18th century; extensive cross-index in Smith (1960), 205ff, which should incl.: Let's be merry and banish thinking (Poro); Love's a dear deceitful jewel (Water Music, minuet); Love thou great ruler (Siroe); The birds no more shall sing (Acis and Galatea); Wine's a mistress gay and easy (Ottone).

English hymns

First words (Title)	Remarks
O love divine, how sweet thou art (Desiring to Love)	all *GB-Cfm; words C. Wesley; tunes known respectively as Fitzwilliam, Gopsall and Cannons; all ed. S. Wesley (London, 1826)
Rejoice, the Lord is King (On the Resurrection)	
Sinners obey the Gospel word (The Invitation)	

Italian songs

(numerous arias in GB-Cfm, Lbm[R], intended for operas or cantatas, not listed)

First words	Voice	Remarks
6 songs:		
Son d'Egitto	S	*GB-Lcm* 257; spurious; from G. Bononcini's opera *La regina creduta re* (1706)
Aure, più non bacciate	A	
Porta la braccia al seno	A	
Gran guerrier di tua virtù	A	
Quanto dolci, quanto cari	A	
Non posso dir di più	S	
Di godere ha speranza	high	probably authentic; songsheet (c1719) with alternative Eng. words (see Oh, my dearest, my lovely creature in 'English songs'); also in The Monthly Mask of Vocal Music (Dec 1719)
È troppo bella, troppo amorosa	A	from Ho fuggito amore, see 'Solo cantatas with continuo'

French songs

First words	Remarks
7 items:	
Sans y penser, chanson	**GB-Lbm[R]*; copy with autograph words *D-MÜs*; copy *F-Pc*; copyist's bill for 'una cantata francese', 22 Sept 1707; autograph indicates the last 6 items grouped as a 'Cantate françoise'; ed. in Raugel (1959) [from *F-Pc* copy]; ed. P. Young (Kassel, 1972)
S'il ne falloit [recit]	
Petite fleur brunette, air	
Vous, qui m'aviez procuré [recit]	
Nos plaisirs seront peu durable, air	
Vous ne sauriez flatter [recit]	
Non, je ne puis plus souffrir, air	
2 songs:	
Sans y penser, chanson	autograph sold Sotheby's, London, 13 April 1954
Quand on suit l'amoureuse loix, chanson	
Lorsque deux coeurs d'un tendre feu	listed in Smith (1960), 181, as by Handel; melody resembles Air and Variations from kbd suite in E (see 'Keyboard', 148); probably spurious
Par les charmes d'un doux mensonge	'Air d'Hindil' in Ballard: Les parodies nouvelles et les vaudevilles inconnus, vii (Paris, 1737), 77, spurious

German songs

First words	Remarks
9 arias (B. H. Brockes):	S, [vn], bc; 1724–7; **GB-Lbm[R]*; texts from Irdisches Vergnügen in Gott, i (Hamburg, 1721 and 2/1724); ed. H. Roth (Munich, 1921)
Künft'ger Zeiten eitler Kummer	
Das zitternde Glänzen der spielenden Wellen	
Süsser Blumen Ambraflocken	

Süsse Stille, sanfter Quelle
Singe, Seele, Gott zum Preise
Meine Seele hört im Sehen
Die ihr aus dunkeln Grüften
In der angenehmen Büschen
Flammende Rose, Zierde der Erden
Der Mund spricht zwar gezwungen Nein (Air en langue allemand)
Dank sei dir, Herr

3 songs:
Ein höher Geist muss immer höher denken
Endlich muss man doch entdecken
In deinem schönen Mund

autograph sold Sotheby's, London, 13 April 1954; ? version of aria from Almira with same text

spurious: pubd (London, 1906) as from unspecified cantata; ? intended as insertion in Ger. version of Israel in Egypt; ? forgery by Siegfried Ochs
S, 2 vn, va, 2 ob, bc: spurious; by J. Mattheson (in opera Henrico IV)

Spanish songs

Dizente mis oyos (Air en langue espagnole)

autograph sold Sotheby's, London, 13 April 1954 (facs. in catalogue); see No se emenderá jamás ('Solo cantatas with instruments')

ORCHESTRAL

Orchestral concertos

(scoring given as 'concertino: ripieno' where appropriate)

[6] Concerti grossi, op.3 (London, 1734; rev. 2/c1734; 3/1741) [probably compiled from existing material: no known autographs of movts not otherwise identifiable]

50, 93

50, 51, 83, 94ff

Twelve Grand Concertos in 7 Parts, op.6 (London, 1740), *GB-Cfm, *Lbm[R], copies Lbm, Mp

Op.	Key	Scoring	Remarks	HG	HHA
3 no.1	B♭	2 rec, 2 ob, 2 bn, vn; 2 vn, 2 va, vc, bc	GB-Cfm, Lbm	xxi, 3	iv/11, 3
3 no.2	B♭	2 ob, 2 vn, 2 vc; 2 vn, va, 2 vc, bc	Cfm, Lbm; MSS of Brockes Passion begin with 1 or 2 movts	xxi, 15	iv/11, 25
3 no.3	G	fl/ob, 2 vn; str, bc	Lbm[R]; movts from anthem My song shall be alway, 'Chandos' Te Deum, kbd fugue, G (see 'Keyboard', 231)	xxi, 27	iv/11, 49
3 no.4	F	2 ob, bn, str, bc	Cfm, Lbm[R], Lbm: in some MSS as ov. to Queen Anne Birthday Ode; movt 1 as 'Second overture in Amadis', in 6 Overtures fitted to the Harpsichord, iii (London, 1728) and probably incl. in Amadigi, 20 June 1716; 1st edn. of op.3 has different conc. here. see 'Spurious orchestral'	xxi, 36	iv/11, 65
3 no.5	d	2 ob, str, bc	Lbm[R], Lbm; movts from Chandos anthems In the Lord put I my trust and As pants the hart	xxi, 45	iv/11, 79

Op.	Key	Scoring	Remarks	HG	HHA	
3 no.6	D/d	org/hpd, 2 ob, bn; str, bc	movt 1 used in Ottone, pr. in Otho an Opera (London, 1723); movt 2: copy Lbm[R], R.M. 18.c.6, f. 5–8 (printed version has spurious extra bar)	xxi, 54	iv/11, 93	
6 no.1	G	2 vn, vc; str, bc	29 Sept 1739; 2 ob added later	xxx, 1	iv/14, 3	51
6 no.2	F	2 vn, vc; str, bc	4 Oct 1739; 2 ob added later	xxx, 16	iv/14, 29	
6 no.3	e	2 vn, vc; str, bc	6 Oct 1739	xxx, 31	iv/14, 55	
6 no.4	a	2 vn, vc; str, bc	8 Oct 1739	xxx, 46	iv/14, 73	
6 no.5	D	2 vn, vc; str, bc	10 Oct 1739; 2 ob added later: arr. from ov. to Ode for St Cecilia's Day	xxx, 60	iv/14, 91	
6 no.6	g	2 vn, vc; str, bc	15 Oct 1739; 2 ob added later	xxx, 77	iv/14, 119	
6 no.7	Bb	2 vn, vc; str, bc	12 Oct 1739	xxx, 95	iv/14, 153	
6 no.8	c	2 vn, vc; str, bc	18 Oct 1739	xxx, 107	iv/14, 169	
6 no.9	F	2 vn, vc; str, bc	[26] Oct 1739; movts arr. from org conc., F, 2nd Set no.1, and ov. to Imeneo	xxx, 118	iv/14, 185	
6 no.10	d	2 vn, vc; str, bc	22 Oct 1739	xxx, 133	iv/14, 205	
6 no.11	A	2 vn, vc; str, bc	30 Oct 1739; arr. from org conc., A, 2nd Set no.2	xxx, 148	iv/14, 225	
6 no.12	b	2 vn, vc; str, bc	20 Oct 1739	xxx, 168	iv/14, 251	
—	C	2 vn, vc; 2 ob, str, bc	25 Jan 1736, Cfm, *Lbm[R], Lbm, Mp; perf. with Alexander's Feast, 19 Feb 1736; pubd in Select Harmony, iv (London, 1740)	xxi, 63	iv/15, 51	
—	Bb	vn; 2 ob, str, bc	c1707, *Lbm[R]; entitled 'Sonata a 5'	xxi, 108	iv/12, 29	
—	Bb	ob; str, bc	?early work; pubd in Select Harmony, iv (London, 1740); known as oboe conc. no.1	xxi, 85	iv/12, 17	
—	Bb	ob; str, bc	pubd in Select Harmony, iv (London, 1740); Chandos anthem ovs. (O come let us sing, I will magnify) combined and transposed; known as oboe conc. no.2	xxi, 91	iv/12, 47	
—	g	ob; str, bc	?1703; ed. (Leipzig, 1863) from unknown source: known as oboe conc. no.3	xxi, 100	iv/12, 3	
—	F	2 ob, 4 hn, bn, str, bc with org	c1746, *Lbm[R]; version of ov. to Fireworks Music	xlvii, 72		
—	D	2 ob, bn, 4 hn, 2 tpt, timp, str, bc with org	c1746, *Lbm[R], Mp; version of ov. to Fireworks Music	xlvii, 80		

Six Concertos, op.4 (London, 1738)
A Second Set of Six Concertos (London, 1740) [pubd in kbd transcrs. only; 4 are transcrs. of orch concs. op.6 nos.1, 5, 6 and 10]
A Third Set of Six Concertos, op.7 (London, 1761)
Scoring given as 'solo instruments; ripieno'; parenthesized nos. in Op. column refer to G. F. Händel: Orgel Konzerte, ed. M. Seiffert (Leipzig, 1921)

Organ, harp and harpsichord concertos

Op.	Key	Scoring	Remarks	MS sources	HG	HHA	
4 no.1 (1)	g/G	org; 2 ob, str, bc	1st perf. with Alexander's Feast, 19 Feb 1736	GB-Cfm, *Lbm[R], Lbm, Mp	xxviii, 3	iv/2, 2	50, 95, 96

4 no.2 (2)	Bb	org; 2 ob, str, bc	Cfm, *Lbm, Mp	? 1st perf. with Esther, 5 March 1735	xxviii, 22	iv/2, 36	50, 95, 96
4 no.3 (3)	g	org; vn, vc; 2 ob, str, bc	Cfm, *Lbm, Mp	? 1st perf. with Esther, 5 March 1735; also with different finale without org, see HHA iv/2, 116; also with altered solo part	xxviii, 33	iv/2, 54	50, 95, 96
4 no.4 (4)	F	org; 2 ob, 2 vn, bc	Cfm, *Lbm, Mp	orig. with Alleluia chorus, completed 25 March 1735; perf. with Athalia, 1 April 1735; chorus ed. in HG, xx. 164	xxviii, 43	iv/2, 72	50, 95, 96
4 no.5 (5)	F	org; 2 ob, str, bc	Cfm, *Lbm, Mp	arr. from rec sonata op.1 no.11; ? perf. with Deborah, 26 March 1735	xxviii, 58	iv/2, 94	50, 95, 96
4 no.6 (6)	Bb	harp; 2 rec, 2 vn, bc	Cfm, *Lbm[R]. Lbm, Mp	perf. in Alexander's Feast, 19 Feb 1736; pubd as org conc.	xxviii, 63	iv/2, 104	50, 95, 96
— (13)	F	org; 2 ob, str, bc	*Lbm[R], Lbm, Mp	2nd Set no.1: 1st perf. with Israel in Egypt, 4 April 1739; later autograph revs. by Handel; incl. in Two Organ Concertos (London, c1761); 'The Cuckoo and the Nightingale'	xlviii, 3	[iv/7]	
— (14)	A	org; 2 ob, str, bc	*Lbm[R], Lbm, Mp	2nd Set no.2: ? 1st perf. with Alexander's Feast, 20 March 1739; see orch conc. op.6 no.11; incl. in Two Organ Concertos (London, c1761)	xlviii, 14	[iv/7]	
7 no.1 (7)	Bb	org; 2 ob, 2 bn, str, bc	*Lbm[R]. Mp	17 Feb 1740; perf. with L'Allegro, 27 Feb 1740; MSS incl. fugue from orch conc. op.6 no.11	xxviii, 73	[iv/8]	51, 96
7 no.2 (8)	A	org; 2 ob, 3 vn, va, bc	*Lbm[R]. Mp	5 Feb 1743; perf. with Samson, 18 Feb 1743	xxviii, 90	[iv/8]	
7 no.3 (9)	Bb	org; 2 ob, 3 vn, va, bc	*Cfm, *Lbm[R]	4 Jan 1751; perf. with Alexander's Feast and The Choice of Hercules, 1 March 1751; 2 versions of movts 1 and 3; 'Hallelujah'	xxviii, 102	[iv/8]	
7 no.4 (10)	d	org; 2 ob, 2 bn, str, bc	*Cfm, *Lbm[R]	movt 3 not in MSS	xxviii, 115	[iv/8]	
7 no.5 (11)	g	org; 2 ob, 3 vn, va, bc	Cfm, *Lbm[R]	31 Jan 1750; finale, not in autograph, ? spurious arr. from op.4 no.3	xxviii, 126	[iv/8]	65
7 no.6 (12)	Bb	org; 2 ob, 3 vn, va, bc	*Cfm, *Lbm[R]	perf. 1749; orig. as orch suite without org, not completed as such	xxviii, 135	[iv/8]	
— (15)	d	org; 3 vn, va, bc	*Lbm[R]	ed. S. Arnold: The Works of Handel (London, 1797)	xlviii, 57	iv/12, 69	
— (16)	F	org; ?2 ob, str, bc	*Lbm	c1748; arr. of Concerto a due cori no.3; HG follows spurious version in Arnold's edn; see also 'Keyboard', 188	xlviii, 68		
—	A	org; str, bc	*Lbm[R]	pastiche conc.: movts from 2nd Set no.2, op.4 no.6, op.7 no.2	—		
—	d	org; 2 ob, 2 bn, va, 2 vc, db, org	†*Cfm	?c1738; movt used for op.7 no.4	xlviii, 51	iv/12, 87	
—	G	hpd; 2 ob, str, bc	*Cfm	c1739; final ritornello and orch bass added to kbd chaconne (see 'Keyboard', 229); ed. T. Best in Chaconne in G for Keyboard (London, 1979)	—		

Concerti a due cori
(HG refers to 2/1894; each includes 2 wind choirs)

No.	Key	Scoring	Remarks	HG	HHA
1	Bb	2 ob, bn; 2 ob, bn; str, bc	c1747, *GB-Lbm[R], *Lbm: ? perf. with Joshua, 9 March 1748; movts arr. from Alexander Balus, Messiah, Belshazzar, Ottone, Semele and Lotario	xlvii, 130	iv/12, 97
2	F	2 ob, 2 hn, bn; 2 ob, 2 hn, bn; str, bc	c1747, *Lbm[R]: ? perf. with Alexander Balus, 23 March 1748; movts arr. from Esther, Messiah and Occasional Oratorio	xlvii, 159	
3	F	2 ob, 2 hn, bn; 2 ob 2 hn, bn; str, bc	c1747, *Cfm, *Lbm[R], Mp: ? perf. with Judas Maccabaeus, 1 April 1747; movt arr. from Partenope; later arr. as org conc., F, c1748; see also 'Keyboard', 188	xlvii, 203	96

Suites and overtures
(printed works published in London)

Title, Key	Scoring	MS sources	Remarks	HG	HHA
Overture, Bb	2 ob, str, bc	GB-Lbm[R]	?1707; in Overtures, 11th Collection (1758); ? orig. ov. to Il trionfo del Tempo e del Disinganno, 1707, see Mainwaring (1760), p.57	xlviii, 108	iv/15, 3
Sinfonia, Bb	2 vn, bc	D-DS	—	—	iv/15, 13
Suite des pieces, F	2 ob, 2 hn, 2 vn, va ad lib, bc	*GB-Lbm[R]	c1737-8; only movt 1 extant, related to ov. to Chandos anthem, O come let us sing	xxi, 98	iv/12, 63
Water Music: Suite, F	2 ob, 2 hn, str, bc	*Lbm	c1716-17; 2 movts, related to Water Music presumably all or part perf. during royal procession on River Thames, 17 July 1717; 2 minuets in A General Collection of Minuets (1729); 9 nos. pubd (by 1734); complete suites arr. hpd (c1760); in score in Arnold edn., vols. xxiii-xxiv (1788); orig. order of movts uncertain	xlvii, 2	iv/13, 97
Suite, D	2 ob, bn, 2 hn, str, bc; 2 ob, bn, 2 tpt, 2 hn, str, bc	Cfm, Lbm, Mp		xlvi, 18	iv/13, 3
Suite, G	rec, fl, str, bc				35, 93
Overture, D: (i) —	2 ob, bn, 3 vn, va, bc; fl, vn, str, bc	*Lbm[R]	c1722-3; movt 1 probably separate frag.; movts 2-3 ? intended to follow concerto movt used in Ottone (1723), i.e. 1st movt of orch conc. op. 3 no.6		iv/15, 43
(ii) Adagio					
(iii) Allegro	2 ob, str, bc				
Water Piece, D	tpt, str, bc	Lbm	(1733); authenticity uncertain; movts arr. from Water Music and Partenope	—	iv/13, 106
Overture, F	2 ob, 2 hn, str, bc	*Lbm[R]	c1734; movts used in ovs. to Il Parnasso in festa and Il pastor fido (1734)	xlviii, 141; lxxxiv, 70	
Sinfonia, Bb	ob, 3 vn, va, bc	*Lbm[R]	c1745, inc.; used for org conc. op.7 no.6 and introduction to Joshua	—	

150

Title, Key(s)	Scoring	Source	Remarks	HG	HHA	
Sonata [Concerto], g	ob, 2 vn, bc	Malmesbury family's private collection	c1717: last movt version of kbd fugue (see 'Keyboard', 194)		iv/15, 29	
Music for the Royal Fireworks, D	3 [24] ob, 2 [12] bn, 3 [9] tpt, 3 [9] hn, [3] timp [str, bc]	*Lbm[R]*	perf. 27 April 1749 for Peace of Aix-la-Chapelle (1749); movt 1 orig. for doubled wind only, str added in autograph and pubd parts; other movts originally for wind and str but str cancelled in autograph	xlvii, 100	iv/13, 61	64, 65, 93, 96

Other orchestral
(in GB-Lbm[R] unless otherwise stated)

Title, Key(s)	Scoring	Remarks	HG	HHA
Marches		see 'Music for wind ensembles'		
Minuets	tr inst, bc	24 minuets out of 60 in A General Collection of Minuets made for the Balls at Court (London, 1729) appear not to derive from other works; others in R.M. 18.b.8 and elsewhere	ii, 143 (1); xlviii, 140 (1)	—
Minuet, D	tr inst, bc	*GB-Cfm 263, 80: 'for his Majesty's Birth Day', in Select Minuets, ii (London, 1745), 17, and Handel's Favourite Minuets (London, 1762), 62	—	
Minuet, D	tr inst, bc	*Cfm 259, 24: 'for the Prince of Wales's Birth Day', in Select Minuets, ii (London, 1745), 35	—	
Gigue, Bb	str, bc	*Cfm 262, 37	—	
Coro and [Bourrée], Bb; Allemande, g; Rigadon, d; Allemande, G; Bourrée, g; [Minuet], g; Allemande, G	2 ob, bn, str, bc	R.M. 18.b.8, ff.62v–69v; ? dances from Daphne; rigadon and 2nd bourrée, 2 ob, bn, in Rigaudon, Bourrée and March, ed. K. Haas (London, 1958)	—	
Minuet and Coro, Bb; Sarabande, F: Gavotte, g	str, bc	R.M. 18.b.8, ff.75–6; ? dances from Florindo; kbd version of minuet, sarabande and gavotte on ff.96r, 4r, 4v, ed. in Pieces for the Harpsichord (London, 1928), nos.72, 23, 4	—	
Allegro, G	2vn, bc	Cfm 798 (Barrett-Lennard x)	xlviii, 140	
Aria [Hornpipe], c	str, bc	R.M. 19.a.4, f.21; kbd version R.M. 18.b.8, f.70v, ed. in Pieces for the Harpsichord (London, 1928), no.52	—	
Hornpipe, D	vn, va, bc	BENcoke, Lbm[R]; for Vauxhall concert, 1740	xlviii, 144	
Hornpipe, G	unspecified	Lbm Add.29371, f.76v; tune entitled 'Hendal's Hornpipe' = Air VI in Act 3 of C. Coffey: The Female Parson, April 1730; also in J. Rutherford: Compleat Collection of 200 ... Country Dances, i (London, c1756), 35, and elsewhere; authenticity uncertain	—	

Spurious orchestral

(scoring given 'solo: ripieno' where appropriate)

Title, Key	Scoring	Remarks
Forest Music, D		see 'Doubtful sonatas'
Concerto, F	vn; 2 ob, str, bc	in 1st edn. of op.3 as no.4, replaced in later edns.; repubd anon. in Select Harmony, iii (London, 1735); ed. in HHA iv/11, 105
Concerto, b	va; 2 fl, 2 vn, 2 va, vc, db	'realised and orchestrated' and ?written by H. Casadesus (Paris, 1925)
Concerto, E♭	ob; str, bc	S-Uu; ed. F. Zobeley (Brunswick, 1935); by R. Woodcock
Concerto, D	2 vn; 2 hn, 2 vn, bc	D-RH 616: ed. M. Seiffert (Leipzig, 1939); ed. in HHA iv/12, 131
Concerto, g	rec, 2 ob, bn, str, bc	PA Fü 274Iα; ed. J. P. Hinnenthal (Bielefeld, 1952)
Concerto, D	fl, str, bc	DS; ed. A. Hoffmann (Wolfenbüttel, 1954); spurious arr. of 4 arias from Flavio
Suite, D	tpt. 2 ob, 2 bn. str. bc	PA Fü 17 (unattrib.); ed. J. P. Hinnenthal (Bielefeld, 1955), attrib. Handel

MUSIC FOR WIND ENSEMBLES

(mostly for military wind ensembles; not in HG or HHA unless otherwise stated)

A General Collection of Minuets . . . to which are added 12 Celebrated Marches, tr inst, b (London, 1729) [GCM, item no.]
Warlike Musick, tr inst, b (London, 1758) [WM, vol., p. no.]
30 Favourite Marches which are now in Vogue, tr inst (London, c1760) [TFM, p. no.]

Title, Key	Scoring	Remarks
March, F	2 ob, 2 hn, bn	GCM, 3, and WM, ii, 26, both in G; TFM, 13 as 'March in Ptolemy'; incl. in Tolomeo ov. in 6 Overtures . . . in 8 Parts, vi (London, c1740); ed. in HG xlviii, 143
March, G	unspecified	GCM, 5; Ladys Banquet, ii (London, 1733), 21; WM, ii, 28; TFM, 15 as Ld. Loudon's March
March, G	unspecified	GCM, 6; Ladys Banquet, ii (London, 1733), 20; WM, ii, 28; TFM, 18 as Admiral Boscowin's March
March, F	unspecified	GCM. 9: WM. ii, 33
March, C	unspecified	GCM, 11; WM, ii, 36
March, D	tpt, 2 ob, bn	GB-Cfm, Lbm[R], Mp, US-Ws; WM, iv, 74 (in G); in Trio Sonata, op.5 no.2; ed. in HG xlviii, 142
Minuet, G	2 ob, 2 hn, bn	c1745. *Cfm 260. 25; version in Fireworks Music
Minuet, G	2 ob, 2 hn, bn	c1745. *Cfm 263, 77
March, G	2 ob, 2 hn, bn	c1745. *Cfm 263. 26; version in Judas Maccabaeus
March, D	tpt, 2 ob, bn	c1746. *Cfm 263. 55; WM, iv, 74 as Dragoon's March
March, D	2 ?ob, 2 ?hn, bn	c1746. sketch *Cfm 263, 78 (hn 2); WM, iv, 73; related to chorus in Alexander Balus
March for the Fife, D	[fife], b	c1747. *Cfm 259. 61; version of chorus from Joshua
March for the Fife, C	[fife], b	c1747. *Cfm 259, 61; version of introduction to Joshua
Music for the Royal Fireworks		see 'Suites and overtures'

153

2 Arias, F	2 ob, 2 hn, bn	Lbm[R] R.M. 18.b.8, ff. 25r–32; i: arr. of Benché tuoni (Teseo); ii: frag. *C/m 260, 22; ed. K. Haas (London, 1958)

2 Arias, F — 2 ob, 2 hn, bn — Lbm[R] R.M. 18.b.8, ff. 25r–32; i: arr. of Benché tuoni (Teseo); ii: frag. *C/m 260, 22; ed. K. Haas (London, 1958)

Rigadon, d, and Bourrée, g — 2 ob, bn — Lbm[R] R.M. 18.b.8. ff.65r–66v; i: version of dance in Almira; ed. K. Haas (London, 1958): probably part of orch suite; see 'Other orchestral'

March, G — 2 ob, bn — *C/m 263, 57: ed. K. Haas (London, 1958) [with above]

Ouverture [Suite], D — 2 cl, hn — c1742; *C/m 264, 17–23; ed. J. M. Coopersmith and J. LaRue (New York, 1950; ed. K. Haas (London, 1952); ed. in HHA iv/15, 85

March, C — unspecified — ?authentic; WM, iv, 77, and TFM, 9, both as Handel's March

March, D — [2 ob, bn] — 2 versions in WM, ii, 29 and iv, 76, both as Grenadier's March; 2nd version in trio sonata, op.5 no.2

Duo, F — 2 [rec] — *C/m; ed. T. Dart (London, 1948); see Trio sonatas, no.19

SONATAS

[12] Sonates, tr inst, bc [op.1] (? London, Walsh, c1730), rev. as [12] Solos [op.1] (London, c1732) [c1730 edn. pubd under probably false imprint of Roger, 91 Amsterdam]

VI sonates, 2 tr insts, bc, op.2 (? London, Walsh, c1730), rev. as VI sonates, op.2 (London, c1732–3) [c1730 edn. pubd under probably false imprint of 91 Roger, Amsterdam; no autographs known, copies D-B, Dlb, DK-Kk, GB-BENcoke, C/m, Lbm[R], Lcm, Mp]

Seven Sonatas or Trios, 2 vn/fl, bc, op.5 (London, 1739) [copies D-B, GB-Lbm[R]; mostly reworkings of existing music] 50, 91

Trio sonatas

No.	Op.	Key	Scoring	Remarks	HG	HHA
1	2 no.1	b	fl/vn, vn, bc	HG, op.2 no.1b; most MSS have ?orig. version in c; see no.14	xxvii, 92	iv/10/1, 3
2	2 no.2	g	2 vn, bc	in GB-Mp copy: 'Compos'd at the Age of 14'	xxvii, 105	iv/10/1, 15
3	2 no.3	B♭	2 vn, bc	HG, op.2 no.4; related to ov. to Esther and org conc. op.4 no.2	xxvii, 115	iv/10/1, 23
4	2 no.4	F	fl/rec/vn, vn, bc	HG, op.2 no.5; related to ovs. to Chandos anthems O sing unto the Lord, O come let us sing, and ov. to Il Parnasso in festa	xxvii, 122	iv/10/1, 35
5	2 no.5	g	2 vn, bc	HG, op.2 no.6; related to org conc. op.4 no.3	xxvii, 128	iv/10/1, 45
6	2 no.6	g	2 vn, bc	HG, op.2 no.7	xxvii, 136	iv/10/1, 61
7	5 no.1	A	2 vn, bc	movts from ov. to Chandos anthem I will magnify and Arianna ballets; new movts, C/m Barrett-Lennard, x	xxvii, 156	iv/10/2, 3
8	5 no.2	D	2 vn, bc	movts from ov. to Chandos anthem O be joyful and Ariodante ballets; for movts 6–7 see Marches in 'Music for wind ensembles'	xxvii, 156	iv/10/2, 11
9	5 no.3	e	2 vn, bc	movts from ov. to Chandos anthem As pants the hart, Terpsicore/Il pastor fido and Ariodante ballets, and Ezio; new movt, C/m 798 (Barrett-Lennard, x)	xxvii, 166	iv/10/2, 19
10	5 no.4	G	2 vn, bc	movts from ovs. to Athalia and Il Parnasso in festa, Il pastor fido, 1734, and Alcina ballets	xxvii, 172	iv/10/2, 29
11	5 no.5	g	2 vn, bc	*Lbm[R]; movts from Terpsicore, and arr. from Tamerlano, Athalia and 2 kbd fugues (see 'Keyboard', 83, 163); movt 6 ?not new	xxvii, 182	iv/10/2, 49

(margin ref. at no.7: 92)

No.	Op.	Key	Scoring	Remarks	HG	HHA
12	5 no.6	F	2 vn, bc	*Cfm, *Lbm[R]; 2 movts based on no.15: pubd version has orig. finale replaced by minuet (copy: Mp)	xxvii, 188	iv/10/2, 63
13	5 no.7	Bb	2 vn, bc	movts from ovs. to Chandos anthems Let God arise and O sing unto the Lord, Oreste ballets and Terpsicore	xxvii, 195	iv/10/2, 75
14	—	c	rec/fl, vn, bc	HG, op.2 no.1a: ?orig. version of op.2 no.1	xxvii, 99	iv/10/1, 113
15	—	F	2 vn, bc	HG, op.2 no.3: D-Dlb; see op.5 no.6	xxvii, 109	iv/10/1, 73
16	—	g	2 vn, bc	HG, op.2 no.8: Dlb; authenticity uncertain	xxvii, 142	iv/10/1, 85
17	—	E	2 vn, bc	HG, op.2 no.9; Dlb; authenticity doubtful	xxvii, 148	iv/10/1, 99
18	—	e	2 fl, bc	GB-Lbm[R] R.M.19:a.4, ff.22–30; ed. F. Nagel (Mainz, 1971); authenticity uncertain	—	
19	—	F	2 rec, bc	movts 2 and 3 *Cfm 261, 72–76, ed. T. Dart as Grave and Allegro (London, 1951); full version in US-Wc M350. M3 Case, ed. C. Hogwood (London, 1981); upper parts of movt 1 identical with Duo in F (see 'Music for wind ensembles')	—	
20	—	C	2 vn, bc	*Cfm 259, 1–13, version of ov. to Saul, ?sketch for ov. not independent work	—	Critical Commentary, i/13, 107–13, 161–3

91

HWV 405

Solo sonatas (with bc)

Editions: The complete Sonatas for Treble (Alto) Recorder & Continuo, ed. D. Lasocki and W. Bergmann (London, 1979) [RLB]
The Three Authentic Sonatas for Oboe and Basso Continuo, ed. D. Lasocki (London, 1979) [OL]

No.	Key	Solo inst	MS sources	Remarks	HG	HHA
1	a	rec	*GB-Lbm[R]	op.1 no.4; RLB no.2	xxvii, 15	iv/3, 21
2	Bb	rec	*Cfm	ed. T. Dart, Fitzwilliam Sonatas (London, 1948), no.1; RLB no.5	—	iv/18, 15
3	C	rec	*Cfm, Mp	op.1 no.7; movt 3 = version of no.10, movt 3; RLB no.3	xxvii, 25	iv/3, 33
4	d	rec	*Cfm, Mp	pubd in b for fl as op.1 no.9, HG xxvii, 32, HHA iv/3, 42; ed. K. Hofmann (Neuhausen, nr. Stuttgart, 1974); RLB no.6	—	iv/18, 19, 45
5	F	rec	*Cfm, Mp	op.1 no.11; see org conc., op.4 no.5; RLB no.4	xxvii, 40	iv/3, 52
6	g	rec	*Cfm, Mp	op.1 no.2; movts 2 and 4 also in no.7; RLB no.1	xxvii, 9	iv/3, 16

No.	Key	Scoring	Source	Remarks	HG	HHA
6a	D	fl	B-Bc: Litt. XY.15, 115 'Sonata XXX'	attrib. 'Sr Weisse (J. S. Weiss?) but probably Handel's, c1707; see Lasocki and Best (1981)	—	iv/18, 41
7	e	fl	*Lbm[R]	ed. in HG as op.1 no.1a; 2 movts adapted from no.13, 1 from no.6a; 2 movts transposed from no.6	xxvii, 2	iv/3, 2
8	Bb	ob	*Cfm	ed. A. H. Mann (London, c1892), for fl; ed. T. Dart (London, 1948), for ob; OL no.2	—	iv/18, 29
9	c	ob	*Cfm, Mp	op.1 no.8; OL no.1	xxvii, 29	iv/18, 32
10	F	?ob	B-Bc, GB-Mp, T 1131. f.120	frag. of movt 3 *Cfm; pubd for fl, in G, as op.1 no.5, HG xxvii, 19, HHA iv/3,28; see no.3; OL no.3	—	iv/18, 36
11	A	vn	*Cfm, Mp	op.1 no.3	xxvii, 12	iv/4, 2
12	D	vn	*Lbm[R]	c1750; inc. in HG as op.1 no.13	xxvii, 47	iv/4, 28
13	d	vn	*Cfm, Mp	pubd for fl, in e, as op.1 no.1, HG xxvii, 6, HHA iv/3. 10	—	iv/18, 10
14	G	vn	*Cfm	ed. K. Hofmann (Neuhausen, nr. Stuttgart, 1974), for rec	—	iv/18, 3
15	g	vn	*Cfm, Mp	pubd for ob as op.1 no.6	xxvii, 22	iv/18, 6
16	g	va da gamba	*Cfm	adaptation of no.15, authorized by autograph; ed. T. Dart (London, 1950)	—	
17	A	vn	*Cfm	?sketch for orch movt; ed. R. Howat, with no.4, as Fantasia and Sonata (London, 1976)	—	
18	a	[vn]	*Cfm, 260, 18	frag., 1 movt	—	
19	c	[vn]	*Cfm, 260, 19-20	frag.; 1 movt; related to 4th movt of no.1 and 4th movt of Trio sonata no.2; ed. in RLB. Appendix	—	

Unaccompanied instrumental solo

Allegro, G (*Cfm 262. 55, dated in pencil 1738) appears to be intended as a prelude for unacc. vn.

Doubtful and spurious sonatas

92

No.	Key	Scoring	Remarks	HG	HHA
1	Bb	ob, vn, hpd	GB-Lbm[R]; no.1 of 6 sonatas, c1696, cited as Handel's earliest music; attrib. doubtful	xxvii, 58	iv/9. 3
2	d	ob, vn, hpd	no.2 of 6 sonatas, as no.1	xxvii, 63	iv/9, 13
3	Eb	ob, vn, hpd	no.3 of 6 sonatas, as no.1	xxvii, 68	iv/9, 23
4	F	ob, vn, hpd	no.4 of 6 sonatas, as no.1	xxvii, 74	iv/9, 35
5	G	ob, vn, hpd	no.5 of 6 sonatas, as no.1	xxvii, 80	iv/9, 45
6	D	ob, vn, hpd	no.6 of 6 sonatas, as no.1	xxvii, 84	iv/9, 53
7	g	2 fl, hpd	Lcm 260; no.1 of 3 sonatas added to MS following 4 genuine sonatas; ed. J. A. Parkinson, attrib. Handel (London, 1969); spurious	—	

No.	Key	Scoring	Remarks	HG	HHA
8	D	2 fl, hpd	no.2 of 3 sonatas, as no.7	—	
9	e	2 fl, hpd	no.3 of 3 sonatas, as no.7; in J. J. Quantz: 6 sonatas, op.3 (London, 1733)	—	
10	d	fl, vn, vc, hpd	attrib. Handel, *D-WD*, ed. F. Zobeley as Concerto a 4 (Mainz, 1935); attrib. Telemann, *Dlb*, *DS*; spurious	—	
11	D	2 vn, va, hpd	as no.10	—	
12	g	vn, va da gamba, bc	*DK-Kk*; ed. M. Seiffert (Leipzig, 1934); spurious	—	
13	F	ob, bn, bc	*D-PA*; ed. M. Seiffert (Leipzig, 1938); spurious	—	
14	Bb	ob, vn, bc	*PA*; ed. W. Hinnenthal (Kassel, 1949); spurious	—	
15	g	ob, vn, bc	*F-AG*; ed. W. Kolneder (Mainz, 1965); spurious		
16	A	vn, bc	op.1 no.10, doubtful; in HG as op.1 no.14	xxvii, 51	iv/4, 46
17	E	vn, bc	op.1 no.12, doubtful; in HG as op.1 no.15	xxvii, 54	iv/4, 55
18	g	vn, bc	rev. op.1 no.10, doubtful	xxvii, 37	iv/4, 28
19	F	vn, bc	rev. op.1 no.12, doubtful	xxvii, 42	iv/4, 40
20	a	fl, bc	doubtful; no.1 of Six Solos, Four for a German Flute … Compos'd by Mr Handel, Sigr Geminiani, Sigr Somis, Sigr Brivio (London, 1730)	xlviii, 130	iv/3, 57
21	e	fl, bc	doubtful: no.2 of Six Solos, Four for a German Flute (London, 1730): movts 1–2 from no.9 of 'Solo sonatas'; movt 4 = kbd minuet, g, see 'Keyboard', 242	xlviii, 134	iv/3, 63
22	b	fl, bc	*GB-BENcoke*, doubtful: no.3 of Six Solos, Four for a German Flute (London, 1730)	xlviii, 137	iv/3, 68
23	C	va da gamba, hpd	*D-DS*, spurious; ? by J. M. Leffloth (1705–31), see A. Einstein, *SIMG*, iv (1902–3), 170	xlviii, 112	
24	G	vn, bc	*LEm*, spurious; ed. M. Seiffert (Leipzig, 1924)	—	
25	D	fl, bc	*PA*, spurious; no.5 of J. J. Quantz: Solos for a German Flute [op.1] (London, 1730); misattrib. Handel in *PA*, ed. W. Hinnenthal (Kassel, 1949, 2/1960 with correct attrib.)	·	
26	g	2 vn, bc	*GB-Mp* ('not Handel's'); ed. S. Flesch (Kassel, 1976)	—	
27	G	fl, bc	*B-Bc* Litt. XY. 15, 115 'Sonata xxvii', spurious; ed. R. Kubik (Kassel, 1980); see Lasocki and Best (1981)	—	
Forest music	D	vn, bc	ed. W. Ware (Dublin, c1803); *GB-Lcm*; all 3 movts arr. from anon. hn duets in Forrest Harmony, ii (1733); probably spurious	—	

All probably for hpd and written before 1720, unless otherwise stated; substantial differences exist between contemporary printed sources and MSS, many of which have variant orderings; secondary MS sources excluded.

KEYBOARD

Editions: A Third Set of Lessons for the Harpsichord, ed. S. Arnold (London, c1793) [vols.cxxx–cxxxi of Arnold edn.] [A]

Pieces for the Harpsichord, ed. W. B. Squire and J. A. Fuller Maitland (London, 1928) [B]

Unbekannte Meisterwerke der Klaviermusik, ed. W. Danckert (Kassel, 1930) [D]

The Young Pianist's Händel, i, ed. M. Aldridge (London, 1969) [P]

Pieces à un & deux clavecins (Amsterdam, Roger, ?1721) [based on pre-1720 sources] [Roger]

Suites de pieces pour le clavecin, i (London, 1720) [partly new, partly earlier material]; HG ii, 1–60; HHA iv/1 [1720]

Prelude et chaconne avec LXII variations, op.1 (Amsterdam, ?1732) [1732¹]

Sonata pour le clavecin, op.2 (Amsterdam, ?1732) [1732¹]

Capriccio pour le clavecin, op.3 (Amsterdam, ?1732) [1732¹]

Preludio et allegro pour le clavecin, op.4 (Amsterdam, ?1732) [1732¹]

Fantasie pour le clavecin, op.5 (Amsterdam, ?1732) [1732¹]

Suites de pieces pour le clavecin, ii (London, 1733) [?unauthorized print of material from Roger excluded from 1720, and other items]; HG ii, 63–122; HHA iv/5 [1733]

Six Fugues or Voluntarys, op.3 (London, 1735); HG ii, 161–74; HHA iv/6, 1–23 [1735]

Autograph MS locations are listed by *RISM* sigla; MS anthologies are listed as follows:

a – lost MS (formerly in Barrett-Lennard collection), partly transcr. M. R. Lacy,
    GB-Lbm Add.31573, ff.33–51, and by Chrysander, HG xlviii, 146–75

b – *US-NYp* Drexel 5856

c – *GB-Lbm* Add.31577

d – *Mp* 130 Hd4 v.268

e – *D-B* 9161/H.2

f – *B* 9162/3

g – *B* 9164/1

h – *B* 9164/3

i – *B* 9168	
j – *GB-Lbm* R.M.18.b.4	
k – *Lbm* R.M.18.b.8	
l – *Lbm* R.M.19.a.3	
m – *Lbm* R.M.19.a.4	
n – *BENcoke* Rivers MS	
o – *BENcoke* Wesley MS	
p – *BENcoke* Walond MS	
x – formerly E. M. Ripin's private collection	
y – Malmesbury family's private collection (3 MSS)	

No.	Key	Title	MS sources (autographs; anthologies)	First published (contemporary; subsequent)	Remarks	HG	HHA
1	A	Suite:		1720, no.1		ii,1	iv/1, 2
		Prelude	x, y				
2		Allemande	x, y		rev. for 1720		
3		Courante	x, y				
4		Gigue	x, y				
5	A	Air	*GB-Lbm*[R]			—	iv/6, 58
6	A	Allemande	*Cfm*			—	iv/6, 50
7	A	Passepied	m	B i, 15		—	
	A	Suite (Partita)			? transcr. of orch dance see under 'Doubtful and spurious'		
8		Allemande					
9		Courante					
10		Sarabande					
11		Gigue					

No.	Key	Title	MS sources (autographs; anthologies)	First published (contemporary; subsequent)	Remarks	HG	HHA
15	a	Prelude	j	B i, 38		—	iv/17, 106
16	a	Allegro	j, x	B i, 39		—	iv/17, 107
17	a	Fugue	Lbm[R]; k, l, y	1735, no.5		ii, 171	iv/6, 17
18	a	Prelude	Lbm[R]		paired with 19 in HG	ii, 140	iv/6, 67
19	a	Lesson		A, 9	2 copies in T 1131, 1 in g	ii, 140	iv/6, 68
20	a	Sonatina	k, x	B ii, 33	HHA disputes authenticity	—	iv/17, 134
21	a	Allemande	k	B ii, 32		—	iv/17, 86
25	b	Suite (frag.): Allemande	Lbm[R]; y		version of 118	—	iv/5, 102
26		Courante	y			—	iv/17, 130
27	b	Fugue	k, l, y	1735, no.4		ii, 168	iv/6, 12
30	Bb	Suite: [Prelude]	b, d, p, y	1733 [no.7] see 34	= 34	ii, 97;	iv/5, 56,
		Allemande	a, b, c, d, m, n, p, x, y	Roger, 40; 1733, 47	2 versions	xlviii, 146	112
31		Courante	a, c, m	Roger, 41; 1733, 48		ii, 98	iv/5, 58
32		Sarabande	a, b, c, d, m, p, x, y	Roger, 42; 1733, 49	2 versions	ii, 99; xlviii, 147	iv/5, 59, 113
33		Gigue	a, c, m, x	Roger, 42; 1733, 50		ii, 99	iv/5, 60
	Bb	Suite:		1733 [no.1]	modern edns. erroneously incl. 242 here		
34		Prelude	BENcoke; c, x	Roger, 55; 1733, 1	before 30 in some MSS; 2 versions	ii, 63	iv/5, 1
35		Sonata (Allegro)	BENcoke; b, c, l, x, y	Roger, 56; 1733, 3	autograph is frag. of early version	ii, 64	iv/5, 2
36	Bb	Air (with 5 variations)	b, c, l, p, x, y	Roger, 58; 1733, 5	2 versions	ii, 66	iv/5, 5
37	Bb	Fugue	Lbm[R]; k, l, y	1735, no.3		ii, 166	iv/6, 9
38	Bb	Air	k, x	B ii, 16	for 2-manual hpd		iv/17, 124
39	Bb	Air	k, n	B ii, 26	in G as no.10 of A General Collection of Minuets (London, 1729)		iv/17, 118
40	Bb	Sonatina	Cfm; n			ii, 150	iv/6, 56
50	C	Suite: Prelude [and Fugue]	f	D, 17		—	iv/17, 1
51		Allemande	f				
52		Courante	f				

No.	Key	Title	MSS	Printed source	Remarks	Ref. 1	Ref. 2
53		Sarabande [and Double]	f			—	iv/17, 10
54		Gigue	f		version of 126		
55	C	Chaconne (with 49 variations)	b, f, l, p, y	B i, 22	D incl. version with 26 variations, from MS anthology f, as part of above suite		
	C	Sonata:	Cfm (draft), Lbm[R] (fair copy)		c1750; ? orig. for musical clock	ii, 154	iv/6, 60
56		Allegro					
57		Trio			version of 268		
58		Gavotte					
59	C	Sonata		1732²: The Ladys Banquet, v (London, c1734)	version of finale of orch conc., C in A Collection of Lessons ... by Dr Greene, ii (c1755), but probably Handel's	ii, 151	iv/6, 24
60	C	Fantasia		1732²: The Ladys Banquet, v (c1734)		ii, 133	iv/6, 35
62	C	Air	Cfm	P i, 2	see Mann (1964–5)	—	
63	C	Passepied	Cfm	B ii, 63	version of 91, related to finale of Radamisto; see Mann (1964–5)	—	
64	C	Prelude (Allegro)	m	B i, 19		—	iv/17, 52
	c	Suite:			for 2 kbd, 1 part lost; reconstruction in Suite for Two Keyboards, ed. T. Dart (London, 1950)	xlviii, 162	
70		Prelude [Allemande]	a, b, c, d, o, y				
71		Courante	a, b, c, d, o, y				
72		Sarabande	a, b, c, d, o, y				
73		Chaconne	a, b, c, d, o, y	D, 40	version of 81		iv/17, 96
	c	Suite (Partita):					
74		Prelude	h				
75		Allemande	h				
76		Courante	h		version of 80		
77		Gavotte	h				
78		Menuet	h			—	iv/17, 101
	c	Suite:					
79		Prelude	k	B ii, 27		—	
80		Allemande	k	B ii, 27	version of 75		
81		Courante	k	B ii, 30	version of 72		
82	c	Air	m	B i, 20			iv/17, 138
83	c	Fugue	Lbm[R]; k, l, y	1735, no.6	HHA disputes authenticity	ii, 173	iv/6, 21

No.	Key	Title	MS sources (autographs; anthologies); Cfm	First published (contemporary; subsequent)	Remarks	HG	HHA
90	D	March		P i, 4	version of 63, derived from finale of Radamisto	—	
91	D	Passepied	k	B ii, 54		—	
95	d	Suite: Overture	a			xlviii, 170	iv/17, 60
96		Allemande	a, i				
97		Courante	a, i				
98		Sarabande I, II	a, i				
99		Chaconne (with 10 variations)	a				
100	d	Suite: Prelude	a, e			xlviii, 152	iv/17, 68
101		Allemande	a, e		version of 277		
102		Courante	a, e				
103		Sarabande	a, e				
104		Air (with 7 variations)	a, e		version of 116		
105		Gigue	a, e				
106		Menuet	a, e				
107	d	Suite: Prelude	a, b, c, d, p, y	1733 [no.4]	partly used in 112	xlviii, 149	
108		Allemande	a, b, c, d, p, y	Roger, 1		ii, 81	iv/5, 29
109		Courante	a, b, c, d, p, y	Roger, 2; 1733, 25		ii, 82	iv/5, 30
110		Sarabande (with 2 variations)	a, b, c, d, p, y	Roger, 3; 1733, 26		ii, 82	iv/5, 31
111		Gigue	a, b, c, d, y	Roger, 4; 1733, 27		ii, 83	iv/5, 33
112	d	Suite: Prelude	Lbm[R]; k, y	Roger, 4; 1733, 28; 1720, no.3	new for 1720 (partly from 107)	ii, 12	iv/1, 18
113		Allegro [Fugue]	Cfm (2 copies)		orig. independent; rev. for 1720		
114		Allemande	Lbm[R]		new for 1720		
115		Courante			new for 1720		
116		Air (with 5 variations)	b, c, d, p, x, y		version of 104; rev. for 1720 from Il pastor fido ov.		
117		Presto			rev. for 1720 from Il pastor fido ov.; many versions		
118	d	Suite: Allemande	l, x, y	1733 [no.3]; 1733, 16	probably post-1720; MSS, Cfm	ii, 75	iv/5, 20
119		Allegro	l, x, y	1733, 18	version of 25		
120		Air [Sarabande]	l, x, y	1733, 19			
121		Gigue	l, x, y	1733, 20			

No.	Key	Title	MS sigla	Printed source	Notes	Ref.	Ref.
122	d	Minuet	k, l, x, y; C/m; d	1733, 22; A, 3	composed 1739 for Princess Louisa; copies, C/m, Lbm[R]	ii, 125	iv/6, 38
123		Suite: Allemande					
124		Courante					
125		Sarabande					
126		Gigue					
127	d	[Hornpipe]	Lbm[R]; m	P i, 11			iv/17, 50
128	d	Prelude	C/m; b, d, y	B i, 17			iv/6, 55
129	d	Prelude	d, o, y				iv/17, 35
130	d	Prelude	k, n, x				iv/17, 128
131	d	Sonata (Allegro)	a, b, c, d, i, p, y	B ii, 50			iv/17, 84
132	d	Sonatina	k		follows 111 in many MSS	xlviii, 150	
133	d	Prelude		B ii, 45		—	
145	E	Suite: Prelude		1720, no.5	new for 1720, replacing 149	ii, 32	iv/1, 44
146		Allemande	b, x, y		3 versions, incl. rev. for 1720		
147		Courante	b, x, y		3 versions, incl. rev. for 1720		
148		Air (with 5 variations; 'Harmonious Blacksmith')	y		2 versions, incl. rev. for 1720; see also 230		
149	E	Prelude	b, y		see 145	—	
150	E	Fugue		ed. H. D. Johnstone (London, 1974)	copy, Lco	—	
151	E	Sarabande/Minuet	1	B i, 37	see B. Matthews, ML, xlii (1961), 131 for facs. of autograph	—	
160	e	Suite: Allemande	b, l, x, y	1733 [no.5]; Roger, 10; 1733, 29		ii, 84	iv/5, 34
161		Sarabande	b, l, x, y	Roger, 11; 1733, 30			
162		Gigue	b, l, x, y	Roger, 12; 1733, 31	2 versions		
163	e	Suite: Allegro [Fugue]	k, y	1720, no.4	orig. independent; inc. autograph of another version, Lbm	ii, 24	iv/1, 34
164		Allemande	C/m; b, x, y	Roger, 14	new version for 1720		
165		Courante	b, x, y	Roger, 14			
166		Sarabande	C/m; b, x, y	Roger, 16	ending rev. for 1720		
167		Gigue	b, x, y	Roger, 17			
175	F	Suite/Sonata: Adagio	x, y	1720, no.2; Roger, 43	rev. for 1720	ii, 6	iv/1, 10
176		Allegro	x, y	Roger, 44			
177		Adagio	x, y	Roger, 45			

No.	Key	Title	MS sources (autographs; anthologies)	First published (contemporary; subsequent)	Remarks	HG	HHA
178		Allegro [Fugue]	Cfm; x, y	Roger, 46		ii, 142	iv/5, 76
179		Allegro	Cfm; x, y	Roger, 49; 1733, 64 (in G)	not in 1720; as prelude to 228 in 1733	—	
180	F	Air	Cfm		version of Air in Water Music	—	iv/13, 97
181	F	Air (with 2 variations)	k, n	B ii, 48		—	iv/17, 126
182	F	Allemande	Cfm		c1730–35		iv/6, 51
183	F	Capriccio				ii, 144	iv/6, 28
184	F	Chaconne	l, o, y	1732?; The Ladys Banquet, v (c1734)	for 2-manual hpd	ii, 136	iv/17, 54
185	F	Fugue	k, y	A, 16 (2 staves); B ii, 18 (4 staves)		—	iv/17, 87
186	F	Gigue	Cfm	B ii, 42		—	iv/6, 54
187	F	Prelude	k	P i, 17		—	iv/17, 119
188	F	Concerto	Cfm, Lbm	B ii, 41	ed. F. Hudson as Concerto in Judas Maccabaeus (Kassel, 1976)		
	f	Suite:			c1748; org part of concerto (arr. from Concerto a due cori no.3) adapted for solo perf.		
193		Prelude	Lbm[R]	1720, no.8		ii, 54	iv/1, 72
194		Fugue	Lbm[R]; k, y		new for 1720		
195		Allemande	b, c, y	Roger, 50	orig. independent		
196		Courante	b, c, y	Roger, 51			
197		Gigue	b, c, y	Roger, 53	rev. for 1720		
198	f	Prelude	c, k	B ii, 41	orig. preceded 195		iv/17, 120
	f♯	Suite:		1720, no.6			
204		Prelude				ii, 39	iv/1, 54
205		Largo	Lbm[R]; b, c, x, y		new for 1720, replacing 208		
206		Allegro [Fugue]	b, c, x, y		from fugue in ov. to In the Lord put I my trust		
207		Gigue	Lbm[R]; b, c, x, y		2 versions		iv/6, 57
208	f♯	Prelude	Lbm[R]; b, c, y		orig. preceded 205	—	iv/17, 27
	G	Suite (Partita):		D, 34			
211		Prelude	g				
212		Allemande	g				
213		Courante	g				
214		Sarabande	g				
215		Gigue	g				

No.	Key	Title		Sources	Prints	Remarks	HG	HHA
216	G	Minuet	g		1733 [no.8]		ii, 100	iv/5, 61
217		Suite:	b		1733, 51			
		Allemande						
218		Allegro			1733, 52			
219		Courante			1733, 54			
220		Aria			1733, 56			
221		Minuet			1733, 57			
222		Gavotte			1733, 59			
223		Gigue			1733, 62			
224	G	Prelude and Capriccio: Prelude		a, e	ed. E. Rimbault: The Pianoforte (London, 1860), 340	see Pestelli (1972)	xlviii, 166	iv/17, 38
225		Capriccio/Toccata		a, b, e, l, x, y				
226	G	Concerto: Allegro		k, n, x	B i, 59	version of sinfonia in Scipione, Act 3	—	iv/17, 114
227		Andante		k, x	B i, 62	version of Andante in orch conc., op.3 no.4	—	iv/17, 116
228	G	Chaconne (with 62 variations)		b, d, p, y	1732?: 1733, 65	preceded in 1732? by part of fantasia by W. Babell (HG xlviii, 230; HHA iv/5, 114), and in 1733 by 179 in G	ii, 110	iv/5, 77
229	G	Chaconne (with 20/21 variations)		b, c, e, l, n, p, x, y	Roger, 18; 1733, 9	2 versions in MSS; prints have different versions with omissions; 2 authentic versions ed. T. Best as Chaconne in G for Keyboard (London, 1979)	ii, 69	iv/5, 11
230	G	Chaconne/Aria (with 5 variations)		b, c, d, p, x, y		2 versions; see 148 for other versions in E	—	iv/6, 4
231	G	Fugue		Lbm[R]; k, l, y	1735, no.2	orch version as finale to orch conc., op.3 no.3	ii, 163	iv/6, 4
232	G	Sonata		j	Roger, 60; B ii, 4		—	iv/6, 80
233	G	Gavotte		m	B i, 15		—	
234	G	Sonatina (Fuga)		Cfm; k	B ii, 46	for 2-manual hpd	—	iv/6, 56
241	g	Overture: Ouverture		b, c, y	Roger, 34	version of ov. to cantata Cor fedele; rev. as 250	—	
242	g	Suite: Minuet		b, c, k, p, y	Roger, 36; 1733, 8		ii, 68	iv/5, 10
243	g	Prelude		b, c, d, x, y	Roger, 6	in a in Roger; other sources in g	—	iv/6, 79

No.	Key	Title	MS sources (autographs; anthologies)	First published (contemporary; subsequent)	Remarks	HG	HHA
244		Andante (Sonata)	b, c, n, x, y	Roger, 6	= 251	—	
245	g	Allegro	b, c, n, x, y	Roger, 8	= 252	—	
		Suite:		1733 [no.6]	1733 and modern edns. omit sarabande	ii, 88	iv/5, 40
246		Allemande	a, b, l, y	Roger, 24; 1733, 34			
247		Courante	a, b, l, y	Roger, 26; 1733, 37			
248		Sarabande	a, b, y	Roger, 28	2 versions; rev. as 253	xlviii, 148	
249		Gigue	a, b, j, l, o, y	Roger, 28; 1733, 40; other versions: B i, 41, 44	3 versions		iv/5, 106, 108
	g	Suite:		1720, no.7			
250		Ouverture	see 241	see 241	241 rev. for 1720	ii, 45	iv/1, 61
251		Andante	see 244	see 244	= 244		
252		Allegro	see 245	see 245	= 245		
253		Sarabande	see 248	see 248	248 rev. for 1720		
254		Gigue	b, c, y		orig. independent; rev. for 1720		
255		Passacaille (Chaconne)	b, c, d, n, y	Roger, 37	orig. independent		
	g	Suite:					
256		Ouverture	a (frag.), m	B i, 8	? transc. of orch items	—	
257		Entrée	m	B i, 10		—	iv/17, 44
258		Menuets I, II	m	B i, 11		—	iv/17, 46
259		Chaconne	m	B i, 12			iv/17, 47 ; iv/6, 42
	g	Suite:	Cfm; d	A Favourite Lesson (London, c1770)	composed 1739 for Princess Louisa; copies, Cfm, Lbm[R]	ii, 128	
260	g	Allemande					
261		Courante					
262		Sarabande					
263		Gigue					
264	g	Fugue	Lbm[R]; k, l, y	1735, no.1		ii, 161	iv/6, 1
		Prelude and Allegro:		1732⁴, The Ladys Banquet, v (c1734)		ii, 148	iv/6, 32
265		Prelude					
266		Sonata (Allegro)					
267	g	Air	k, m	B ii, 13	for 2-manual hpd	—	iv/17, 122
268	g	Air	k, x	B i, 52	version of 57	—	iv/17, 109
269	g	Bourée ('Impertinence')	k	B ii, 46			iv/17, 126
270	g	Capriccio	Cfm	Lessons by Handel (London, ?1787), 10	c1720	ii, 131	iv/6, 48

		Title			
271	g	Chaconne	k	B ii, 36	iv/17, 90
272	g	Prelude	j	B i, 41	iv/17, 120
273	gg	Sonata	k	B i, 58	iv/17, 113
274	g	Sonatina	k	B i, 54	iv/17, 112
275	g	Sonatina	Lbm[R]	P i, 5	c1749–50: basis of In gentle murmurs (Jephtha)
276	gg	Toccata	k	B i, 53	iv/17, 110
277	g	Suite (frag.): Allemande			copy: A-Wm XIV 743, f.34 version of 101
278		Courante			
279	g	Prelude on Jesu meine Freude			pr. in Mann (1964 5)

Doubtful and spurious

(probably spurious, unless otherwise stated; only published works listed)

Title, key	Remarks
Suite, a	*GB-BENcoke* Aylesford MS. without attrib.: minuet attrib. Handel in Pièces de clavecin de Mr Handel (Paris, ?1739) and Recueil de pièces … accomode pour les flûtes travers, i (Paris, c1738), and attrib. Loeillet. *Lbm* Add.31577, ff.18v–19r: minuet, transposed to g, pubd as theme of Pastorale et théme avec variations, harp/pf (Vienna, 1826), attrib. Handel; ed. H. J. Zingel (Mainz, 1956) [without pastorale]
Ten Select Voluntaries for the Organ or Harpsichord … by Mr Handel, Dr Green etc, ii (London, ?1771)	not individually attrib.; almost certainly none by Handel
Twelve Voluntaries and Fugues for the Organ or Harpsichord with Rules for Tuning by … Mr Handel, iv (London, c1780)	not individually attrib.: incl. 6 'little' fugues, ed. in HG xlviii, 183–90
'Microcosm' Concerto, Bb	attrib. Handel in Musical Remains … selected … Edward Jones (London, 1796); by John Jones (London, 1848), arr. M. R. Lacy
Grand March, G	?partly authentic; pubd as Partita … d'apres le manuscrit de J. Chr. Smith (Leipzig, 1864); MS. now lost; sold London, June 1860; see Chrysander (1858–67), iii, 200, and preface to
Partita, A	HG xlviii; ed. in HG xlviii, 176, HHA, iv/6, 70; see AMZ, new ser., i (1863), no.38, col.652; no.39, cols 665f
Sonatina, d; Allemande, g	attrib. Handel, *D-Hs*'s 146, ff.6r, 45v, with Allemande attached to Suite, g (see 'Keyboard', 250–55); ed. T. W. Werner, Deutsche Klaviermusik aus dem Beginne des 18. Jahrhunderts (Hanover, 1927)
'Schicksalfuge', f	ed. K. Anton (Halle, 1940); repr. in W. Serauky: 'Karl Loewe als Händel-Verehrer', Händel-Festspiele (Halle, 1958), 38
12 fantasias, 4 pieces	*CH-Zz*; ed. G. Walter, Zwölf Fantasien und vier Stücke für Cembalo (Leipzig and Zurich, 1942); incl. Sonata, C (see 'Keyboard', 59), other items probably spurious
2 preludes and fugues, C	kbd. 4 hands; ed. H. Schüngeler, Zwei Fugen (Magdeburg and Leipzig, 1944); by J. Marsh

Title, key	Remarks
Concerto, F; Preludes, Capriccios, Introduzione, Allemande, Badinage, Canzone	H-Bn, ed. F. Brodszky, Cembalodarabok (Budapest, 1964); incipit of Badinage, HG xlviii, p.VII
Air, c	GB-Lbm Add.31467, f.10v; ed. in HHA iv/17, 133

HARP MUSIC

Except for a sinfonia in Saul, there is no authentic music for unacc. harp; for the spurious Pastorale et thème see 'Keyboard: Doubtful and spurious'. Suite, a. For harp conc., see 'Orchestral: organ, harp and harpsichord concertos'.

CLOCK MUSIC

(c1735–45, known only in 2 MSS; all in one movement; ed. in W. B. Squire, 1919)

Title, key	Remarks
Set I: F, C, C, C, F, C, C, G, C, C, C	'Tunes for Clay's Musical Clock': GB-Lbm R.M.19.a.1, ff.160–71; no.2 = variant of Set II no.3; no.4 = arr. of Vola l'augello (Sosarme); no.5 = arr. of Lungo pensar (Muzio Scevola); no.6 = arr. of Alla fama (Ottone); no.7 = arr. of Deh lascia un tal desio (Arianna); no. 8 = arr. of last movt of Scipione ov.; no.9 = arr. of Del onda ai fieri moti (Ottone); no.10 = arr. of In mille dolci modi (Sosarme); no.11 = arr. of In mar tempestoso (Arianna)
Set II: Sonata, C; [untitled], C; A Voluntary or a Flight of Angels, C; [untitled], C; [untitled], a; Menuet, a; Air, a	Lbm R.M.18.b.8, ff.59–60; no.3, see Set I; no.6 = version of Minuet in Almira, g, pubd in Pieces for the Harpsichord, ii (London, 1928), 59

Other works possibly for musical clock incl. Sonata, C (see 'Keyboard', 56–8), and Allegro, C, *C/m 262, 56, dated 25 Aug 1738; incipit in Chrysander (1858–67), iii, 200

DIDACTIC WORKS

Short exx. illustrating fugal procedures and types of figured bass, GB-C/m 260, 27–72; copies of the basses, BENcoke Rivers MS; see Mann (1964–5); ed. (with other, doubtfully related material) in HHA, Supplement Band i (1978)

Bibliography

GENERAL

HJb (1928–33/*R*, 1955–)

K. Taut: 'Verzeichnis des Schriftums über Georg Friedrich Händel', *HJb 1933*

K. Sasse: *Händel Bibliographie* (Leipzig, 1963; suppl., 1967)

W. C. Smith: *A Handelian's Notebook* (London, 1965)

A. Mann and J. M. Knapp: 'The Present State of Handel Research', *AcM*, xli (1969), 4

CATALOGUES, SOURCE MATERIAL

J. A. Fuller Maitland and A. H. Mann: *Catalogue of the Music in the Fitzwilliam Museum, Cambridge* (London, 1893)

A. Hughes-Hughes: *Catalogue of Manuscript Music in the British Museum* (London, 1906–9/*R*1964–6)

R. A. Streatfeild: 'The Granville Collection of Handel Manuscripts', *MA*, ii (1910–11), 208

W. B. Squire: 'Handel in Contemporary Song-books', *MA*, iv (1912–13), 102

Sotheby, Wilkinson and Hodge Sale Catalogue of the Library of W. H. Cummings 17–24 May 1917 (London, 1917)

Sotheby, Wilkinson and Hodge Sale Catalogue of the Collection of the Earl of Aylesford 13 May 1918 (London, 1918)

N. Flower: *Catalogue of a Handel Collection formed by Newman Flower* (Sevenoaks, 1920)

W. B. Squire: *Catalogue of the King's Music Library*, i: *The Handel Manuscripts* (London, 1927)

F. Zobeley: 'Werke Händels in der Gräfl. von Schönbornschen Musikbibliothek', *HJb 1931*, 98

E. H. Fellowes: *The Catalogue of Manuscripts in the Library of St. Michael's College Tenbury* (Paris, 1934)

J. M. Coopersmith: 'Handelian Lacunae: a Project', *MQ*, xxi (1935), 224

——: 'Some Adventures in Handel Research', *PAMS 1937*, 11

W. C. Smith: 'Recently Discovered Handel Manuscripts', *MT*, lxxviii (1937), 312

J. M. Coopersmith: 'Concert of Unpublished Music by Georg Friedrich Händel: Program Notes', *PAMS 1939*, 213

——: 'The First Gesamtausgabe: Dr. Arnold's Edition of Handel's Works', *Notes*, iv (1946–7), 277, 439

P. Hirsch: 'Dr Arnold's Handel Edition', *MR*, viii (1947), 106

G. Kinsky, ed.: *Manuskripte, Briefe, Dokumente von Scarlatti bis Stravinsky: Katalog der Musikautographen-Sammlung Louis Koch* (Stuttgart, 1953)

W. C. Smith: 'Verzeichnis der Werke Georg Friedrich Händels', *HJb*

1956, 125–67 [rev. version of catalogue in *Handel: a Symposium*, ed. G. Abraham (London, 1954)]

F. Hudson: 'Concerning the Watermarks in the Manuscripts and Early Prints of G. F. Handel', *MR*, xx (1959), 7

W. Shaw: *A First List of Word-books of Handel's 'Messiah', 1742–83* (Worcester, 1959)

R. Ewerhart: 'Die Händel-Handschriften der Santini-Bibliothek in Münster', *HJb 1960*, 111–50

W. C. Smith: *Handel: a Descriptive Catalogue of the Early Editions* (London, 1960, rev. 2/1970)

L. W. Duck: 'The Aylesford Handel Manuscripts', *Manchester Review*, x (1965), 228

M. Picker: 'Handeliana in the Rutgers University Library', *Journal of the Rutgers University Library*, xxix (1965), 1

P. Krause: *Handschriften und ältere Drucke der Werke Georg Friedrich Händels in der Musikbibliothek der Stadt Leipzig* (Leipzig, 1966)

J. S. Hall: 'The Importance of the Aylesford Handel Manuscripts', *Brio*, iv/1 (1967), 7

A. H. King: *Handel and his Autographs* (London, 1967)

H. Lenneberg and L. Libin: 'Unknown Handel Sources in Chicago', *JAMS*, xxii (1969), 85

P. J. Willetts: *Handlist of Music Manuscripts Acquired* [by *GB-Lbm*] *1908–67* (London, 1970)

Catalogue of Rare Books and Notes (Tokyo, 1970) [Ohki Collection, Nanki Music Library]

H. D. Clausen: *Händels Direktionspartituren ('Handexemplare')* (Hamburg, 1972)

A. D. Walker: *George Frideric Handel: the Newman Flower Collection in the Henry Watson Music Library* (Manchester, 1972)

J. M. Knapp: 'The Hall Handel Collection', *Princeton University Library Chronicle*, xxxvi (1974), 3

F. Hudson: 'The Earliest Paper Made by James Whatman the Elder (1702–1759) and its Significance in Relation to G. F. Handel and John Walsh', *MR*, xxxviii (1977), 15

B. Baselt: *Thematisch-systematisches Verzeichnis: Bühnenwerke (Händel-Handbuch 1)* (Leipzig, 1978)

——: 'Verzeichnis der Werke Georg Friedrich Händels (HWV)', *HJb 1979*, 10–139

BIOGRAPHIES, BIOGRAPHICAL SOURCES

BurneyH; *HawkinsH*

J. Mattheson: *Grundlage einer Ehren-Pforte* (Hamburg, 1740); ed. M. Schneider (Berlin, 1910/*R*1969)

[J. Mainwaring]: *Memoirs of the Life of the Late George Frederic Handel* (London, 1760/*R*1964, 1967)

J. Mattheson: *Georg Friedrich Händels Lebensbeschreibung* (Hamburg, 1761/*R*1976)

C. Burney: *An Account of the Musical Performances in Westminster Abbey and the Pantheon May 26th, 27th, 29th; and June the 3rd and 5th, 1784: in Commemoration of Handel* (London, 1785/*R*1979)

[W. Coxe]: *Anecdotes of George Frederick Handel and John Christopher Smith* (London, 1799/*R*1980)

H. Townsend: *An Account of the Visit of Handel to Dublin: with Incidental Notices of his Life and Character* (Dublin, 1852)

V. Schoelcher: *The Life of Handel* (London, 1857/*R*1979)

F. Chrysander: *G. F. Händel* (Leipzig, 1858–67/*R*1966); index, S. Flesch (Leipzig, 1967)

M. Delany: *Autobiography and Correspondence of Mary Granville, Mrs Delany* (London, 1861–2)

J. Marshall: *Handel* (London, 1883, 3/1912)

W. S. Rockstro: *The Life of George Frederick Handel* (London, 1883)

J. O. Opel: *Mitteilungen zur Geschichte der Familie des Tonkünstlers Händel* (Halle, 1885)

A. Ademollo: *G. F. Haendel in Italia* (Milan, 1889)

F. Volbach: *Georg Friedrich Händel* (Berlin, 1898, rev. 2/1907, 3/1914)

W. H. Cummings: *Handel* (London, 1904)

R. A. Streatfeild: *Handel* (London, 1909, rev. 2/1910/*R*1964)

——: 'Handel in Italy 1706–10', *MA*, i (1909–10), 1

R. Rolland: *Haendel* (Paris, 1910, rev. 2/1974; Eng. trans., 1916/ *R*1975)

R. A. Streatfeild: 'Handel's Journey to Hanover in 1716', *MA*, ii (1910–11), 119

——: *Handel, Canons and the Duke of Chandos* (London, 1916)

N. Flower: *George Frederic Handel: his Personality and his Times* (London, 1923, rev. 3/1959, with bibliography by W. C. Smith)

H. Leichtentritt: *Händel* (Stuttgart, 1924)

W. C. Smith: 'George III, Handel and Mainwaring', *MT*, lxv (1924), 789

J. M. Coopersmith: 'A List of Portraits, Sculptures, etc. of Georg Friedrich Handel', *ML*, xii (1932), 156

J. Müller-Blattau: *Georg Friedrich Händel* (Potsdam, 1933)

E. J. Dent: *Handel* (London, 1934)

R. W. M. Wright: 'George Frederick Handel: his Bath Associations', *MO*, lviii (1934–5), 846

E. H. Müller, ed.: *The Letters and Writings of George Frideric Handel* (London, 1935)

P. M. Young: *Handel* (London, 1946, rev. 3/1975)

W. C. Smith: *Concerning Handel, his Life and Works* (London, 1948)

A. E. Cherbuliez: *Georg Friedrich Händel: Leben und Werk* (Olten, 1949)

H. and E. H. Mueller von Asow: *Georg Friedrich Händel: Briefe und Schriften* (Lindau, 1949) [incl. Mattheson's trans. of Mainwaring, 1760]

W. C. Smith: 'Handeliana', *ML*, xxxi (1950), 125; xxxiv (1953), 11

W. Siegmund-Schultze: *Georg Friedrich Händel: Leben und Werk* (Leipzig, 1954, rev. 3/1962)

O. E. Deutsch: *Handel: a Documentary Biography* (London, 1955/ *R*1974)

H. Becker: 'Die frühe Hamburgische Tagespresse, als musikgeschichtliche Quelle', *Beiträge zur Hamburgischen Musikgeschichte*, i, ed. H. Husmann (Hamburg, 1956), 22

W. Serauky: *Georg Friedrich Händel: sein Leben, sein Werk* (Kassel, 1956–8) [only iii–v pubd]

W. Braun: 'Beiträge zu G. F. Händels Jugendzeit in Halle (1685–1703)', *Wissenschaftliche Zeitschrift der Martin-Luther-Universität Halle-Wittenberg: Gesellschafts- und Sprachwissenschaftliche Reihe*, viii (1959), 39

J. S. Hall: 'Handel among the Carmelites', *Dublin Review* (1959), no.233, p.121

B. Matthews: 'Unpublished Letters Concerning Handel', *ML*, xl (1959), 261; see also 406

K. Sasse: 'Opera Register from 1712 to 1734 (Colman-Register)', *HJb 1959*, 199

E. Zanetti: 'Handel in Italia', *Approdo musicale* (1960), no.12, pp.3–46

B. Matthews: 'Handel: more Unpublished Letters', *ML*, xlii (1961), 127; see also 395

W. Rackwitz and H. Steffens: *George Frideric Handel: a Biography in Pictures* (Leipzig, 1962)

S. Sadie: *Handel* (London, 1962)

J. Gress: 'Händel in Dresden (1719)', *HJb 1963*, 135

M. Fabbri: 'Nuova luce sull'attività fiorentina di Giacomo Antonio Perti, Bartolomeo Cristofori e Giorgio F. Haendel', *Chigiana*, xxi (1964), 143–90

P. Hamilton: 'Handel in the Papers of the Edinburgh Musical Society (1728–1798)', *Brio*, i (1964), 19

A. Mann: 'Eine Kompositionslehre von Händel', *HJb 1964–5*, 35

P. H. Lang: *George Frideric Handel* (New York, 1966/*R*1977)

U. Kirkendale: 'The Ruspoli Documents on Handel', *JAMS*, xx (1967), 222–73, 518

C. Cudworth: 'Mythistorica Handeliana', *Festskrift Jens Peter Larsen* (Copenhagen, 1972), 161

W. Dean: 'Charles Jennens's Marginalia to Mainwaring's Life of Handel', *ML*, liii (1972), 160

Autograph Letters of George Frideric Handel and Charles Jennens (London, 1973) [Christie's illustrated sale catalogue, 4 July]

C. Timms: 'Handel and Steffani', *MT*, cxiv (1973), 374

Bibliography 171

J. Kerslake: 'The Likeness of Handel', _Handel at the Fitzwilliam_ (Cambridge, 1974), 24

R. Strohm: 'Händel in Italia: nuovi contributi', _RIM_, ix (1974), 152

W. Dean: 'An Unrecognized Handel Singer: Carlo Arrigoni', _MT_, cxviii (1977), 556

W. Siegmund-Schultze, ed.: _Georg Friedrich Haendel: Beiträge zu seiner Biographie aus dem 18. Jahrhundert_ (Leipzig, 1977)

M. Keynes: 'Handel's Illnesses', _The Lancet_, ii (20/27 Dec 1980), 1354

WORKS: GENERAL

G. G. Gervinus: _Händel und Shakespeare: zur Ästhetik der Tonkunst_ (Leipzig, 1868)

E. Prout: 'Handel's Obligations to Stradella', _MMR_, i (1871), 154

——: 'Urio's Te Deum and Handel's Use thereof', _MMR_, i (1871), 139

G. A. Macfarren: 'The Accompaniment of Recitative', _MT_, xv (1872), 687

F. Chrysander: 'Francesco Antonio Urio', _AMZ_, xiii (1878), 513, 529, 545, 561, 577, 625, 641, 657, 785, 801, 817; xvi (1879), 6, 21, 36, 71, 86, 101, 118

E. Prout: 'Handel's Orchestration', _MT_, xv (1884), 12, 69, 138, 193, 256, 326

——: 'The Orchestras of Bach and Handel', _PMA_, xii (1885–6), 23

——: 'Graun's Passion Oratorio and Handel's Knowledge of it', _MMR_, xxiv (1894), 97, 121

J. Bennett: 'Handel and Muffat', _MT_, xxxvi (1895), 149, 667

F. Volbach: _Die Praxis der Händel-Aufführung_ (Charlottenburg, 1900)

J. S. Shedlock: 'Handel's Borrowings', _MT_, xlii (1901), 450, 526, 596, 756

M. Seiffert: 'Franz Johann Habermann', _KJb_, xviii (1903), 81

J. S. Shedlock: 'Handel and Habermann', _MT_, xlv (1904), 805

S. Taylor: _The Indebtedness of Handel to Works by other Composers_ (Cambridge, 1906/R1979)

P. Robinson: _Handel and his Orbit_ (London, 1908/R1979)

M. Seiffert: 'Händels Verhältnis zu Tonwerken älterer deutscher Meister', _JbMP 1908_, 41

——: 'G. Ph. Telemanns _Musique de table_ als Quelle für Händel', _Bulletin de la Société 'Union Musicologique'_, iv (1924), 1

E. J. Dent: 'Englische Einflüsse bei Händel', _HJb 1929_, 1; Eng. trans., _MMR_, lxi (1931), 225

H. Leichtentritt: 'Handel's Harmonic Art', _MQ_, xxi (1935), 208

W. F. H. Blandford: 'Handel's Horn and Trombone Parts', _MT_, lxxx (1939), 697, 746, 794

H. G. Farmer: _Handel's Kettledrums, and Other Papers on Military Music_ (London, 1950)

G. Abraham, ed.: _Handel: a Symposium_ (London, 1954)

J. S. and M. V. Hall: 'Handel's Graces', _HJb 1957_, 25

W. Siegmund-Schultze: 'Das Siciliano bei Händel', _HJb 1957_, 44–73

A. Lewis: 'Handel and the Aria', *PRMA*, lxxxv (1958–9), 95

Händel-Ehrung der Deutschen Demokratischen Republik: Halle 1959

W. Siegmund-Schultze: 'Zu Händels Schaffensmethode', *HJb 1961–2*, 69–136

J. A. Westrup: 'The Cadence in Baroque Recitative', *Natalicia musicologica Knud Jeppesen* (Copenhagen, 1962), 243

W. Siegmund-Schultze: *Georg Friedrich Händel, Thema mit 20 Variationen* (Halle, 1965)

W. Dean: 'Handel and Keiser: Further Borrowings', *CMc*, no.9 (1969), 73

W. Meyerhoff, ed.: *50 Jahre Göttinger Händel-Festspiele* (Kassel, 1970)

S. Wollenberg: 'Handel and Gottlieb Muffat', *MT*, cxiii (1972), 448

H. C. Wolff: 'Händel in Frankreich', *Festschrift der Händel-Festspiele* (Göttingen, 1973), 19

B. Baselt: 'Miscellanea Handeliana', *Der Komponist und sein Adressat*, ed. S. Bimberg (Halle, 1976), 60

A. Hicks: 'Handel's Early Musical Development', *PRMA*, ciii (1976–7), 80

D. Burrows: 'Handel and the Foundling Hospital', *ML*, lviii (1977), 269

W. Dean: 'The Performance of Recitative in Late Baroque Opera', *ML*, lviii (1977), 389

D. R. B. Kimbell: 'Aspekte von Händels Umarbeitungen und Revisionen eigener Werke', *HJb 1977*, 45

E. T. Harris: *Handel and the Pastoral Tradition* (Oxford, 1980)

OPERAS

G. Ellinger: 'Händels *Admet* und seine Quelle', *VMw*, i (1885), 201

R. A. Streatfeild: 'Handel, Rolli, and Italian Opera in London in the Eighteenth Century', *MQ*, iii (1917), 428

C. Spitz: 'Die Oper *Ottone* von Händel und *Teofane* von Lotti', *Festschrift zum 50. Geburtstag Adolf Sandberger* (Munich, 1918), 265

I. Leux: 'Über die "verschollene" Händel-Oper "Hermann von Balcke" ', *AMw*, viii (1926), 439

R. Steglich: 'Die neue Händel-Opern-Bewegung', *HJb 1928*, 71

E. J. Dent: 'Handel on the Stage', *ML*, xvi (1935), 174

J. M. Coopersmith: 'The Libretto of Handel's *Jupiter in Argos*', *ML*, xvii (1936), 289

W. Schulze: *Die Quellen der Hamburger Oper (1678–1738)* (Hamburg, 1938)

J. Eisenschmidt: *Die szenische Darstellung der Opern Händels auf der Londoner Bühne seiner Zeit* (Wolfenbüttel, 1940–41)

H. C. Wolff: *'Agrippina': eine italienische Jugendoper Händels* (Wolfenbüttel, 1943)

E. Dahnk-Baroffio: 'Das Libretto der Oper "Ariadne" ', *Göttinger Händel-Opern Festspiele* (Göttingen, 1946)

H. F. Redlich: 'Handel's *Agrippina*: Problems of a Practical Edition', *MR*, xii (1951), 15

E. Dahnk-Baroffio: 'Zu den Libretti der Händelzeit', *Festschrift der Händel-Festspiele* (Göttingen, 1953), 15

R. Gerber: 'Von Wesen der Händel-Oper', *Festschrift der Händel-Festspiele* (Göttingen, 1953), 5

R. Brockpähler: *Handbuch zur Geschichte der Barockoper in Deutschland* (Emsdetten, 1954)

E. Dahnk-Baroffio: 'Nicola Hayms Anteil an Händels Rodelinde-Libretto', *Mf*, vii (1954), 295

W. Serauky: 'Das Ballett in G. F. Händels Opern', *HJb 1956*, 91

H. C. Wolff: *Die Händel-Oper auf der modernen Bühne* (Leipzig, 1957)

J. M. Knapp: 'Handel, the Royal Academy of Music, and its First Opera Season in London (1720)', *MQ*, xlv (1959), 145

W. Serauky: 'Händel und die Oper seiner Zeit', *HJb 1959*, 27

E. Dahnk-Baroffio: 'Zur Stoffgeschichte des *Ariodante*', *HJB 1960*, 151

L. Finscher: 'Händels "Alceste" ', *Göttinger Händel-Tage 1960*, 10

S. Flesch: 'Händels "Orlando" ', *Festschrift der Händelfestspiele* (Halle, 1961), 42

H. S. Powers: 'Il Serse trasformato', *MQ*, xlvii (1961), 481; xlviii (1962), 73

B. Trowell: 'Handel as a Man of the Theatre', *PRMA*, lxxxviii (1961–2), 17

S. Flesch: 'Einige Bemerkungen zu Händels Oper *Siroe*', *Festschrift der Halle Festspiele 1952–62* (1962), 35

W. Dean: 'Handel's *Giulio Cesare*', *MT*, civ (1963), 402

D. R. B. Kimbell: 'The Libretto of Handel's *Teseo*', *ML*, xliv (1963), 371

W. Dean: 'Handel's *Riccardo primo*', *MT*, cv (1964), 498

P. Tinel: 'Haendel, réformateur de l'opéra et dramaturge de l'oratorio', *Bulletin de l'Académie royale de Belgique: classe des beaux-arts*, xlvi (1964), 78

W. Siegmund-Schultze: 'Händels "Muzio Scevola" ', *Festschrift der Händelfestspiele* (Halle, 1965), 27

E. Dahnk-Baroffio: 'Zum Textbuch von Händels *Flavio*', *Festschrift der Händel-Festspiele* (Göttingen, 1967), 37

W. Dean: 'Handel's *Scipione*', *MT*, cviii (1967), 902

J. M. Knapp: 'Händels Oper Flavio', *Festschrift der Händel-Festspiele* (Göttingen, 1967), 25

——: 'Probleme bei der Edition von Händels Opern', *HJb 1967–8*, 113

W. Dean: 'Handel's *Amadigi*', *MT*, cix (1968), 324

D. R. B. Kimbell: *A Critical Study of Handel's Early Operas* (diss., U. of Oxford, 1968)

——: 'The "Amadis" Operas of Destouches and Handel', *ML*, xlix (1968), 329

J. M. Knapp: 'Handel's *Giulio Cesare in Egitto*', *Studies in Music*

History: Essays for Oliver Strunk (Princeton, 1968), 389

E. Dahnk-Baroffio: 'Die Völkerwanderungsopern und Händels "Olibrio" ', *Festschrift der Händel-Festspiele* (Göttingen, 1969), 29

W. Dean: *Handel and the Opera Seria* (Berkeley and Los Angeles, 1969)

——: 'A Handel Tragicomedy' [*Flavio*], *MT*, cx (1969), 819

J. M. Knapp: 'The Libretto of Handel's "Silla" ', *ML*, l (1969), 68

P. Gülke: 'Zur Einrichtung Händelscher Opernpartituren', *HJb 1969–70*, 87–122

E. Dahnk-Baroffio: 'Händels "Riccardo primo" in Deutschland', *50 Jahre Göttinger Händel-Festspiele*, ed. W. Meyerhoff (Kassel, 1970), 150

W. Dean: 'Handel's Wedding Opera' [*Atalanta*], *MT*, cxi (1970), 705

——: 'Vocal Embellishment in a Handel Aria', *Studies in Eighteenth-century Music: a Tribute to Karl Geiringer* (New York and London, 1970), 151

R. Gerlach and E. Dahnk-Baroffio: 'Über Georg Friedrich Händels Oper Riccardo I', *Festschrift der Händel-Festspiele* (Göttingen, 1970), 75

J. M. Knapp: 'Handel's *Tamerlano*: the Creation of an Opera', *MQ*, lvi (1970), 405

J. M. Knapp and E. Dahnk-Baroffio: 'Titus l'Empereur', *Festschrift der Händel-Festspiele* (Göttingen, 1970), 27

W. Dean: 'Handel's *Ottone*', *MT*, cxii (1971), 955

J. M. Knapp: 'The Autograph Manuscripts of Handel's "Ottone" ', *Festskrift Jens Peter Larsen* (Copenhagen, 1972), 167

W. Dean: 'A French Traveller's View of Handel's Operas', *ML*, lv (1974), 172

J. M. Knapp: 'The Autograph of Handel's *Riccardo primo*', *Studies in Renaissance and Baroque Music in Honor of Arthur Mendel* (Kassel and Hackensack, 1974), 331

R. Strohm: 'Händels Pasticci', *AnMc*, no.14 (1974), 208–67

B. Baselt: 'Zum Parodieverfahren in Händels frühen Opern', *HJb 1975*, 19

W. Dean: 'Handel's *Sosarme*, a Puzzle Opera', *Essays on Opera and English Music in Honour of Sir Jack Westrup* (Oxford, 1975), 115–47

——: 'Twenty Years of Handel Opera', *Opera*, xxvi (1975), 924

R. Strohm: 'Händel und seine italienischen Operntexte', *HJb 1975*, 101–59

W. Dean, ed.: *G. F. Handel: Three Ornamented Arias* (Oxford, 1976)

G. Bimberg: 'Dramaturgische Strukturelemente in den "Ezio"-Opern von Händel und Gluck', *Georg Friedrich Händel als Wegbereiter der Wiener Klassik: Halle 1977*, 41

R. Strohm: 'Handel, Metastasio, Racine: the Case of "Ezio" ', *MT*, cxviii (1977), 901

S. Stompor: 'Die deutschen Aufführungen von Opern Händels in der ersten Hälfte des 18.Jahrhunderts', *HJb 1978*, 31–89

B. Baselt: 'Händel auf dem Wege nach Italien', *G. F. Händel und seine italienischen Zeitgenossen* (Halle, 1979), 10

W. Dean: 'Die Ausführung des Rezitativs in den Opern des Händel–Zeit', *G. F. Händel und seine italienischen Zeitgenossen* (Halle, 1979), 94

R. Strohm: 'Francesco Gasparini, le sue opere tarde e Georg Friedrich Händel', Francesco Gasparini (1661–1727): *I convegno internazionale: Firenze 1977*, 71

A. Kitching: *Handel at the Unicorn* (n.p., 1981)

J. M. Knapp: 'Handel's First Italian Opera: "Vincer se stesso è la maggior vittoria" or "Rodrigo"', *ML*, lxii (1981), 12

W. Dean: 'Händels kompositorische Entwicklung in den Opern der Jahr 1724/25', *HJb 1982*

ORATORIOS, OTHER VOCAL WORKS

F. Chrysander: 'Händels Orgelbegleitung zu Saul', *Jb für musikalische Wissenschaft*, i (1863), 408

——: 'Der Bestand der königlichen Privatmusik und Kirchenkapelle in London, 1710–1755', *VMw*, viii (1892), 514

E. D. Rendall: 'The Influence of Henry Purcell on Handel, Traced in "Acis and Galatea"', *MT*, xxxvi (1895), 293

T. W. Bourne: 'Handel's Double *Gloria Patri*', *MMR*, xxvii (1897), 125

F. Chrysander: *Händels Biblische Oratorien in geschichtlicher Betrachtung* (Hamburg, 1897)

E. Bernoulli: *Quellen zum Studium Händelscher Chorwerke* (Leipzig, 1906)

M. Seiffert: 'Die Verzierung der Sologesänge in Händels *Messias*', *SIMG*, viii (1906–7), 581–615

H. Goldschmidt: 'Zur Frage der vokalen Auszierung Händel'scher Oratorien', *AMz*, xxxv (1908), 380

M. Seiffert: 'Händels deutsche Gesänge', *Festschrift ... Rochus Freiherrn von Liliencron* (Leipzig, 1910/R1970), 297–314

A. Beyschlag: 'Über Chrysanders Bearbeitung des Händel'schen *Messias* und über die Musikpraxis zur Zeit Händels', *Die Musik*, x (1910–11), 143

J. A. Benson: *Handel's 'Messiah': the Oratorio and its History* (London, 1923)

W. B. Squire: 'Handel's *Semele*', *MT*, lxvi (1925), 137

L. Schrade: 'Studien zu Händels *Alexanderfest*', *HJb 1933*, 38–114

E. Bredenfoerder: *Die Texte der Handel-Oratorien*, (Leipzig, 1934)

W. Serauky: *Musikgeschichte der Stadt Halle* (Halle and Berlin, 1940)

E. Völsing: *G. F. Händels englische Kirchenmusik* (Leipzig, 1940)

J. Herbage: *Messiah* (London, 1948)

R. M. Myers: *Handel's Messiah: a Touchstone of Taste* (New York, 1948)

P. M. Young: *The Oratorios of Handel* (London, 1949)

G. Cuming: 'The Text of "Messiah" ', *ML*, xxxi (1950), 226

W. Dean: 'The Abridgement of Handel', *MMR*, lxxx (1950), 178

——: 'The Dramatic Element in Handel's Oratorios', *PRMA*, lxxix (1952–3), 33

W. Braun: 'B. H. Brockes' "Irdisches Vergnügen in Gott" in den Vertonungen G. Ph. Telemanns und G. Fr. Händels', *HJb 1955*, 42–71

R. M. Myers: *Handel, Dryden and Milton* (London, 1956)

J. P. Larsen: *Handel's Messiah: Origins, Composition, Sources* (London, 1957, rev. 2/1972)

W. Serauky: 'G. F. Händels lateinische Kirchenmusik', *HJb 1957*, 5

H. C. Wolff: 'Die Lucretia-Kantaten von Benedetto Marcello und Georg Friedrich Händel', *HJb 1957*, 74

W. Braun: 'Echtheit und Datierungsfragen im vokalen Frühwerk Georg Friedrich Händels', *Händel-Ehrung der Deutschen Demokratischen Republik: Halle 1959*, 61

——: 'Zur Choralkantate "Ach Herr, mich armen Sünder" ', *HJb 1959*, 100

W. Dean: *Handel's Dramatic Oratorios and Masques* (London, 1959)

L. Finscher: 'Händels "Belsazar" ', *Göttinger Händelfestspiele 1959*, 16

J. S. Hall: 'The Problem of Handel's Latin Church Music', *MT*, c (1959), 197

W. Rackwitz: 'Die Herakles-Gestalt bei Händel', *Händel-Ehrung der Deutschen Demokratischen Republik: Leipzig 1959*, 51

F. Raugel: 'Händels französische Lieder', *Händel-Ehrung der Deutschen Demokratischen Republik: Halle 1959*, 115

E. Zanetti: 'A proposito di tre sconosciute cantate inglesi', *RaM*, xxix (1959), 129

R. Ewerhart: 'New Sources for Handel's *La Resurrezione*', *ML*, xli (1960), 127

L. Finscher: 'Händels "Il trionfo del Tempo" ', *Göttinger Händelfestspiele 1960*, 8

——: 'Händels "Englische Kantaten" ', *Göttinger Händelfestspiele 1962*, 32

W. Shaw: *The Story of Handel's Messiah* (London, 1963)

J. Tobin: *Handel at Work* (London, 1964)

W. Shaw: *A Textual and Historical Companion to Handel's Messiah* (London, 1965)

E. Dahnk-Baroffio: 'Zu Aci e Galatea', *Göttinger Händeltage 1966*, 41

W. Dean: 'Masque into Opera' [*Acis and Galatea*], *MT*, cviii (1967), 605

M. Boyd: 'La Solitudine: a Handel Discovery', *MT*, cix (1968), 1111

A. Hicks: 'Handel's *La Resurrezione*', *MT*, cx (1969), 145

J. Tobin: *Handel's Messiah* (London, 1969)

Bibliography   177

W. Braun: 'Drei deutsche Arien: ein Jugendwerk Händels?', *AcM*, xlii (1970), 248

J. Müller-Blattau: 'Händels Festkantate zur 500-Jahr Feier der Stadt Elbing 1737', *50 Jahre Göttinger Händel-Festspiele*, ed. W. Meyerhoff (Kassel, 1970), 120

B. Trowell: 'Congreve and the 1744 Semele Libretto', *MT*, cxi (1970), 993

W. Dean: 'How Should Handel's Oratorios be Staged?', *Musical Newsletter*, i/4 (1971), 11

A. Hicks: 'Handel and Il Parnasso in festa', *MT*, cxii (1971), 339

J. P. Larsen: 'Handel Studies', *American Choral Review*, xiv (1972), 5–48 [special no.]

J. Schilling: 'Händels Kantate: Il pianto di Maria', *Festschrift der Händel-Festspiele* (Göttingen, 1972), 23

D. Burrows: 'Handel's Peace Anthem', *MT*, cxiv (1973), 1230

A. Geering: 'Georg Friedrich Händels französische Kantate', *Musicae scientiae collectanea: Festschrift Karl Gustav Fellerer* (Cologne, 1973), 126

A. Hicks: 'Ravishing Semele', *MT*, cxiv (1973), 275; see also 696

P. Rogers: 'Dating *Acis and Galatea*', *MT*, cxiv (1973), 792

E. Dahnk-Baroffio: 'Jephtha und seine Tochter', *Festschrift der Händel-Festspiele* (Göttingen, 1974), 54

F. Hudson: 'Das Concerto in Judas Maccabaeus identifiziert', *HJb 1974*, 119

B. Baselt: 'Händel und Bach: zur Frage der Passionen', *Johann Sebastian Bach und Georg Friedrich Händel: 24. Händelfestspiele der Deutschen Demokratischen Republik: Halle 1975*

D. Burrows: 'Handel's Performances of "Messiah": the Evidence of the Conducting Score', *ML*, lvi (1975), 319

H. Frederichs: *Das Verhältnis von Text und Musik in den Brockespassionen Keisers, Händels, Telemanns und Matthesons* (Munich and Salzburg, 1975)

A. Lewis: 'Some Notes on Editing Handel's "Semele" ', *Essays on Opera and English Music in Honour of Sir Jack Westrup* (Oxford, 1975), 79

H. J. Marx: 'Ein Beitrag Händels zur Accademia Ottoboniana in Rom', *Hamburger Jb für Musikwissenschaft*, i (1975), 69

C. A. Price: 'Handel and The Alchemist', *MT*, cxvi (1975), 787

M. R. Brownell: 'Ears of an Untoward Make: Pope and Handel', *MQ*, lxii (1976), 554

A. Hicks: 'Handel's Music for Comus', *MT*, cxvii (1976), 28

H. D. Johnstone: 'The Chandos Anthems: the Authorship of no.12', *MT*, cxvii (1976), 601

G. Beeks: *The Chandos Anthems and Te Deum of George Frideric Handel* (diss., U. of California, Berkeley, 1977)

D. Burrows: 'Handel and the 1727 Coronation', *MT*, cxviii (1977), 469

W. D. Gudger: 'A Borrowing from Kerll in "Messiah" ', *MT*, cxviii (1977), 1038
J. S. M. Mayo: *Handel's Italian Cantatas* (diss., U. of Toronto, 1977)
H. Smither: *A History of the Oratorio* (Chapel Hill, 1977–)
G. Beeks: 'Handel's Chandos Anthems: the "Extra" Movements', *MT*, cxix (1978), 621
B. Cooper: 'The Organ Parts to Handel's "Alexander's Feast" ', *ML*, lix (1978), 159
F. Zimmerman: 'Händels Parodie-Ouvertüre zu Susanna: eine neue Ansicht über die Entstehungsfrage', *HJb 1978*, 19
J. S. M. Mayo: 'Zum Vergleich des Wort-Ton-Verhältnisses in den Kantaten von Georg Friedrich Händel und Alessandro Scarlatti', *G. F. Händel und seine italienischen Zeitgenossen* (Halle, 1979), 31
W. D. Gudger: 'Skizzen und Entwürfe für den Amen-Chor in Händels Messias', *HJb 1980*, 83
B. Baselt: 'Händels frühe Kirchenmusik', *Anthem Ode Oratorium – ihre Ausprägung bei G. F. Händel* (Halle, 1981), 21
G. Beeks: 'Zur Chronologie von Händels Chandos Anthems und Te Deum B-Dur', *HJb 1981*, 89
D. Burrows: *Handel and the English Chapel Royal during the reigns of Queen Anne and King George I* (diss., Open U., 1981)
J. Mayo: 'Einige Kantatenrevisionen Händels', *HJb 1981*, 63
H. Serwer: 'Die Anfänge des Händelschen Oratoriums', *Anthem Ode Oratorium-ihre Ausprägung bei G. F. Händel* (Halle, 1981), 34

INSTRUMENTAL WORKS

F. Chrysander: 'Händels zwölf Concerti grossi für Streichinstrumente', *AMZ*, xvi (1881), 81, 97, 113, 129, 145; xvii (1882), 894
——: 'Händels Instrumentalkompositionen für grosses Orchester', *VMw*, iii (1887), 1, 157–88, 451
M. Seiffert: 'Zu Händels Klavierwerken', *SIMG*, i (1899–1900), 131
W. B. Squire: 'Handel's Clock Music', *MQ*, v (1919), 538
G. Abraham: 'Handel's Clavier Music', *ML*, xvi (1935), 278
F. Ehrlinger: *G. F. Händels Orgelkonzerte* (Würzburg, 1940)
G. A. Walter: 'Unbekannte Klaviercompositionen von G. F. Händel', *SMz*, lxxxii (1942), 141
N. K. Nielsen: 'Handel's Organ Concertos reconsidered', *DAM*, iii (1963), 3
R. Gottlieb: 'Französischer, italienischer und vermischter Stil in den Solosonaten Georg Friedrich Händels', *HJb 1966*, 93
P. F. Williams: 'Händel und die englische Orgelmusik', *HJb 1966*, 51
T. Best: 'Handel's Keyboard Music', *MT*, cxii (1971), 845
C. Hill: 'Die Abschrift von Händels "Wassermusik" in der Sammlung Newman Flower', *HJb 1971*, 75
R. Fiske: 'Handel's Organ Concertos: Do they Belong to Particular Oratorios?', *Organ Yearbook*, iii (1972), 15

G. Pestelli: 'Haendel e Alessandro Scarlatti', *RIM*, vii (1972), 103

S. Sadie: *Handel Concertos* (London, 1972)

S. Flesch: 'Georg Friedrich Händels Trio-Sonaten', *HJb 1972–3*, 139–211

T. Best: 'Handel's Solo Sonatas', *ML*, lviii (1977), 430; see also *HJb 1980*, 115

B. Baselt: 'Muffat and Handel: a two-way Exchange', *MT*, cxx (1979), 904

N. Seifas: 'Die Concerti grossi op.6 und ihre Stellung in Händels Gesamtwerk', *HJb 1980*, 9–58

T. Best: 'Die Chronologie von Händels Klaviermusik', *HJb 1981*, 79

D. Lasocki and T. Best: 'A new flute sonata by Handel', *Early Music*, ix (1981), 307

Index